RAVAGE MY SOUL

A POETRY ANTHOLOGY

RAVAGE MY SOUL

NELSON ALVAREZ DE LA CAMPA

authorHOUSE®

AuthorHouse™
1663 Liberty Drive
Bloomington, IN 47403
www.authorhouse.com
Phone: 1-800-839-8640

Published by AuthorHouse   08/16/2012

ISBN: 978-1-4772-4891-1 (sc)
ISBN: 978-1-4772-4890-4 (e)

Library of Congress Control Number: 2012913090

This book is printed on acid-free paper.

CONTENTS

HOSPITAL FOR HEARTS

A Short Story

After being in this place for almost two weeks he had finally had enough. They had taken his freedom from him, his ability to make simple choices; the orderlies told him when it was time to eat, sleep, smoke. Hell, it was a surprise they didn't have his bowel movements on a strict schedule. He had long accepted the fact that his fate was in the hands of others, but at this moment he couldn't wrap his head around the most recent blow. It had left him decimated. They had taken the one thing he needed most of all. They had taken her away, took their love and condemned it; tried to beat it down into an unrecognizable bloody pulp of hearts. The miserable void that had been momentarily filled with her beautiful essence was now emptier than the darkest abyss. He remembered her hand clasped in his, wished he could still feel it, but all that remained was a clammy wetness that disgusted him. He had stopped showing up at meal time, stopped eating, hoping that this simple defiance would make the doctors see the error of their ways. He really only wanted her back, needed her back. He felt that the stability of his mind depended on it. He didn't need these pills for schizos and psychos. They have the wrong diagnosis. They can take their meds and shove it, he thought to himself.

Since her arrival in the hospital, he had felt like a new person. He had experienced a glorious re-birth, and a happiness long forgotten was beginning to spring forth and rush through his veins helping him more than any cocktail of drugs could. Then they found them out. Perhaps they had been too careless, too affectionate, too lovey dovey. He didn't know that this feeling was what he needed all along; otherwise he may have been more cautious, covert. It was this cherished feeling that they yanked from his bleeding spirit, clouding his soul.

He had not left his room for at least two days, and now he walked over to the small room that contained the shower, toilet, and sink. He twisted the handle on the shower, and water began to flow from the showerhead. He remembered those stupid words the doctors had said to him, like words from an arrogant imbecile reciting outdated rules and regulations from a dusty manual: "We have a no-contact policy here. You have broken the rules, and now the both of you will be separated." He stepped into the shower, not bothering to remove any of his clothes. As the clothes absorbed the water, they felt like weights hanging heavily on his body. "Fuck your rules! Contact is what I need! I needed to hold her hand! Can't you see that? You should change your stupid goddamn policy! It makes no sense to deny us human touch! Please, please don't take her," he had pleaded his case. He curled into a fetal position on the shower floor and began to weep. He whimpered words of indignation and shook violently with each gut-wrenching sob. They had broken him. He began to reminisce on happier times. Mainly he thought about the first day she had walked into his world, bringing with her a divine splendor that eliminated the darkness that had filled his already broken heart.

There he sat at a round table in the activities room of the psych ward at Hillside Hospital. He had been there for three days so far, and at the moment he was pondering with some dismay the bizarre series of events that had landed him there. He was sure of only one thing: all of this could have been avoided had he not taken an 8th of psychedelic mushrooms.

His name was Connor Jacobs, and he had taken the mushrooms on Valentine's Day weekend. Valentine's Day had been approaching quicker than a speeding bullet, and all he could think about was his ex-girlfriend who had been everything to him. About a year and a half had passed since the fateful day came when she decided to end their relationship. This blow devastated the poor boy, the young man, the idiot who expected the *I love you's* to go on forever. It had seemed like one day the horrid word "don't" appeared in the sentence to give birth to a horrible truth that haunted Connor: The words "I don't love you anymore" floated from her sweet pink lips and viciously assaulted Connor's heart. He had longed for her ever since. After the proposition had arisen from an old friend, Connor decided that instead of spending Valentine's Day depressed out his mind, he would opt for just being out of his mind.

It was a sunny Sunday afternoon, with a sky absent of clouds, when Connor consumed an 8th of mushrooms. This was after the house was turned into a safe environment for such endeavors. Connor had received a lengthy exposition on the basic functions of the mushrooms (they were a fungi that poisoned your brain) and how long the effects would last (typically eight hours). He was even given a red bracelet to put on his wrist to remind him while in the depths of his experience, that he was indeed just on a trip. All precautions were carried out meticulously, but no one, not the Mushroom Man nor Ken Kesey with all his knowledge on psychotropic drugs, could have planned for the unthinkable.

He looked at his wrist now and in place of the red bracelet there was a plastic hospital band, stating his name, any allergies he may have, and the date of his admission into the psych ward. He had tried desperately to tear it off, but his efforts were futile. He would need a pair of scissors to cut it off, but they certainly wouldn't give him one here.

Since the consumption of the shrooms he had lost both his shoes, walked shoe-less through a Barnes and Noble, wrecked a movie theater, talked to a dog he thought was God, became convinced he was the messiah, saw a smiling-blue fish in a basement, saw dragons spewing fire, took a barefoot shit in a Wendy's, hypnotized by the tiles below his feet, and last but not least Connor went totally bonkers in an emergency room. This, of course, is not a complete list, just some of the highlights.

Connor sat across from his roomie, Bob. When Connor had first awoken in the hospital he was strapped to the bed and it was Bob who got the nurse to un-strap him. "Take it slow. You had a rough night. Take it easy now," she said amiably, as she started to unfasten the brown leathery straps.

"I can't take it easy," Connor responded gruffly. "I gotta get out of here. There's some kind of mistake."

"Well, now you may as well just relax. You're . . . um . . . not permitted to leave the hospital at this moment."

"What?"

"You're here on a 5150. That means that two doctors have evaluated you as psychologically unfit." She didn't go into more detail, figuring he'd understand soon enough. She smiled sympathetically and said brightly, "Don't worry; we'll get you well again."

"Well again?" Connor couldn't process what he was being told.

"Yeah, honey. Don't fret. Most people, after two weeks they're out of here. Sometimes sooner."

"Two weeks?" Connor said in a daze. "Most people?" He started to drift into a dreamy near-catatonic state. He was just now realizing the seriousness of the situation, the reality of his predicament, and the shock that started to befall him was similar to that of being hit by a bundle of bricks.

"You rest now. It's okay, sweetie," she said gently.

It was a blatant lie disguised as condolence. Things were very very far from okay and were only going to get worse.

Connor had since bonded with Bob. Bob had gotten Connor started on smoking little cigars, Swisher Sweets, which he'd look forward to smoking whenever they let them outside for a 15 minute smoke break. Outside there was a tall metal fence, a picnic table, and a basketball hoop with a broken rim hanging down off of it. They were in a cage even when let outside, but Connor didn't care; he loved to feel the cool air caress his skin, as he studied the expensive cars parked on the other side of the fence. It was during one of these breaks when Bob told Connor why he was in there. Bob was autistic, or had some other mental disability. Though he was in his 30s, he spoke and acted like a child. Bob had had a girlfriend before coming here. One of his best friends had slept with her. In a rage, Bob had fought his friend and killed him accidentally. When Bob told Connor the story through his crooked teeth, there were suppressed tears in his eyes, like his eyes were a dam that would break at any second. As he spoke regretfully, he seldom looked at Connor. When he finished, Connor didn't know what to say. He didn't expect this gentle and naïve soul capable of such atrocities. "I'm sorry about what happened. He wasn't a real friend," was all Connor said, though he wanted to say much more but was incapable of finding the right words.

As Connor and Bob sat, waiting for their table to be called so that they could pick up their lunch, they noticed a women being escorted through the front doors, which were pass the nurse's station. Connor was more than intrigued by the women, he was mesmerized. She was too skinny, with unruly hair of various colors: blond, red, and black strands mixing together yet separating themselves in rebellion at the same time. Her face was long and rectangular with a pointed chin and lined forehead, and her eyes were light brown like the most glorious sap. Her eyes captivated Connor. She looked scared, confused, fragile on the verge of breaking, and Connor had a profound desire to help her in any way that he could. He wanted to hold her and tell her everything would be all right even if it was a lie. For the first time in a while Connor had forgotten all about his former love, and was only thinking about how to proceed with this new one. He knew that by helping her he'd in turn help himself.

Since his admittance into the hospital he had kept with him a marble notebook. On the front was written in jagged letters, "Read at your own risk." In it he wrote his everyday thoughts and his innermost feelings. The new patient became a muse for Connor, and he wrote poems fanatically, hoping to one day share them with her.

First he would have to introduce himself. He had enough difficulty with this prospect in the outside world, let alone in a hospital under the scrutiny of doctors and nurses. *So much pressure*, he thought as butterflies slammed around the walls of his stomach. The opportunity arose a couple days later when she was sitting by her lonesome at a table in the activities room. It was an hour before it was time for sleep, and this time was designated for playing board games, cards, or watching TV. After a while of summoning the courage necessary to approach, playing out various scenarios in his head, and wishing he was someone else, he finally walked over to the table and asked her if he could sit down. She nodded passively, her eyes staring straight ahead of her, affixed on nothing in particular.

"Hey, you want to play a board game?" Connor said awkwardly. "No. I hate board games," she said. "Wanna play Uno?" Connor said desperately. Instead of answering his question she said softly, "Do you see that guy carrying the thesaurus around with him?" Her eyes shifted to the right, gesturing to Connor that the man was behind her. "He won't leave me alone. He's like a stalker, always following me around and trying to talk to me. It's really scary." "Don't worry, I'll protect you." Connor said heroically. "What's with the thesaurus?" "I have no idea. He's just some whack job, I guess." "Well, then this is definitely the place for him," Connor said with a tiny laugh. "It's not so bad here though once you get used to the monotony. The food's even starting to grow on me. I look forward to when they serve cheeseburgers." She looked at him incredulously and said, "Are you serious?" In response he said, "Yeah. My mom's a terrible cook, so I guess anything is better than what she usually makes." In response she said, "I hate this place, and I especially hate the food. All I eat is the yogurt most of the time. You know, this isn't my first time being stuck here." "Oh?" Connor said surprised. "But wait, you're not stuck here. I saw you come in by yourself. You voluntarily came in. They didn't drag you in here strapped to a stretcher like they did me." "I came in for one thing" she sighed slowly, "but they're keeping me here for something else. My name's Ashley by the way. My friends call me Ash." Connor thought this was the coolest nickname imaginable, and he hoped that soon he'd be able to call her by it.

"My name's Connor. Connor Jacobs."

"Are you aware that you have two first names?" Ashley said with a smile. The smile revealed a perfect set of white teeth that brightened the surrounding area, casting an ephemeral glow that Connor wished he could bottle. He wanted nothing more than to see that smile over and over, banishing the darkness for an eternity.

"I am all too aware. It's a pretty dumb name."

"Nah, it's cute," Ashley said flirtatiously.

They continued to talk until the nurses proclaimed it time for bed. Ashley told him that they were keeping her in the hospital, because they thought she was anorexic. "Which is totally ridiculous! I mean, I eat, there's just not any hospital food I like!"

"Well, you are awfully skinny," Connor said timidly. "I could see why they think that." Connor told her that she could afford to gain at least 20 pounds. "Just mirror what I eat and you'll be out of here in no time. Hell, before long you'll be obese," Connor said with a laugh. When Ashley joined him he was thankful.

"So, what's your story?"

"It's a pretty crazy one, you sure you want to hear it?"

"I think I can handle it"

"I'll spare you the part of the story where I took shrooms and tripped for like, 3 weeks. I'm still trying to make sense of that part myself," Connor said pensively. "Let me give you the lowdown on how I ended up here." Connor went on to explain how he was in the emergency room for hours. He was still feeling the effects of the psychedelic mushrooms, and he wanted to be anywhere else but the room that they had stuck him in. In his unstable state of mind he was almost positive they were leaking some kind of strange toxin through the air vents. He also couldn't shake the feeling that something terrible had happened in that particular room; he felt a really bad vibe permeating through his bones. Finally a resident came in and asked him all sorts of silly questions like "Do you think you have super powers?" After hours of lying on a wobbly gurney, it started to occur to him that they were treating him like a crazy person.

"That's when I had the idea, 'Alright! If they're going to treat me like I'm crazy, I'll give them crazy!'" Connor said enthusiastically. "Thinking about it now, it probably wasn't the best of ideas."

"Aw, man what did you do?" Ashley said, truly intrigued.

"I jumped out of the room and started screaming, 'Hey, look at me I'm craaaaazzzy.' Then I grabbed a salad that an orderly that was watching my room was eating, and plopped it on my head, dressing and all. I started yelling 'Hey, look at me, I'm a salad head! I have a salad for a head!'"

Ashley and Connor both started cracking up in unison. It was Connor's first time telling anyone how he had ended up at the psych ward at Hillside hospital, and it felt really good to tell someone, like an anchor being lifted off his chest. Then Connor became very solemn and said, "Pretty soon after that little scene two huge guys grabbed me and brought me back into that horrible room. That room was driving me bonkers. When they turned off the lights in the room, I saw these paint splotches on the wall that almost looked like eyes," Connor paused. "So, I grabbed a pen and started to draw a big smiling face on the wall, making the paint splotches into eyes. It was a truly twisted drawing, but it was all I could do to keep from going mad in a way. Soon after that, I attempted to escape the room one more time, telling them that they couldn't keep me in there any longer; that I wouldn't go back. I was a bit hysterical at this point, on the verge of tears. Before I knew it I was dragged back into the room, and forced down on the bed. Two nurses came in and gave me a shot of Thorazine in each arm. The last thing I remember is them starting to strap me down with those damn leather straps."

"Wow, that's one hell of a story," Ashley said dumbfounded.

"You don't know the half of it," Connor said regretfully. "Now they got me diagnosed as some kind of psychotic schizoid or somethin' . . . ."

"Time for bed!!" came the echoing announcement from the nurses, as they started to clean up the mess of board games and playing cards.

"Well, I guess that's all she wrote," Connor said sadly. Having to go into his sleeping quarters at 10 PM seemed ridiculous, and he usually could not go to sleep until he complained enough that they gave him something to ease him into a thoughtless slumber.

"Goodnight, Connor. It was very nice meeting you. I'll talk to ya tomorrow."

"The pleasure was all mine," he tried to say charmingly. "Goodnight, Ash, and don't let the bed bugs bite."

She smiled wonderfully.

He watched her walk off down the hallway designated for all the women patients. When she vanished from his sight, he felt his heart gradually sink, like a raft in the vast ocean, leaking air out of an unfortunate puncture. That night he didn't even attempt to sleep, as his thoughts were filled with saccharine thoughts of a frail and lovely girl, which was soundly sleeping no more than 100 feet away from him. He wrote in his journal, thoughts of her and poems for her, endlessly, till his hand twitched with pain and his eyes could no longer withstand the force of the sandman. Before entering the world of dreams, he remarked that he could barely remember ever feeling so alive. That night his dreams were shaded with glorious reds, blacks, and blonds, entwining and flowing vibrantly.

The next few days were like the beginnings of a quirky romantic comedy with the unlikely setting of a psych ward. Ashley and Connor became inseparable. One would awaken each morning, waiting for the other to awaken as well. They would normally wait for the other in the activities room, or if the urge was strong enough or if impatience took hold, they would linger at the end of their respective hallways, making sure not to actually step into the others hallway because then they would be seriously reprimanded. There was a hallway full of women's dormitories, and a hallway for the men's, and neither sex could trespass into the others. The hallways formed a wide V shape structure, and at the point of the V was the rectangular nurses' station, sometimes bustling with doctors and nurses, and at others times (especially during the night) there would sometimes be only one or two people occupying it.

Ashley and Connor had talked about hundreds of things since her arrival into the ward, and at times they flirted heavily with each other, but Connor was unsure how to take it. He wanted their platonic relationship to go to the next level, at least emotionally. It was Bob who finally coaxed Connor to stop being such a chicken, and suggested that he read one of the poems he had written about her. After much deliberation he decided on a poem entitled "Let me love."

They were sitting at the table where they had first exchanged their tentative words with one another when Connor began to recite the poem to Ashley:

"You, beautiful girl, have bewitched me
Incandescently red, like the sun's core, burning hotter than fire
I could adore you if you would let me
I could love you if you would return my heavenly gaze
But you won't for the rulers of your soul are not the rulers of mine
Hell and night are those which possess you
I am free and pure in a sinful way
I am innocent yet in the hand of the devil
I am shaken by him because you took my world and twirled it in your hands, shaking me
harder than I've ever been—
Once I've felt like this, when in the grasp of a heavenly angel and all her glory
She saved and tortured me till my last gasping breath only whispered her sweet
melancholy name
But I long to whisper someone else's name
I desire yours to flow from my lips freely as I proclaim all that you are and aren't to me
One day you'll be mine
and one day you'll break my heart
One day I'll kiss your soft tender lips and get lost in your sparkling eyes
and one day you'll send a knife slicing through the vulnerable layers of my skin
One day things will go my way
One day you'll love me like I wish you'd let me love you
I beseech you, let me love you for all that you are, for all that you aren't, for all that I
despise, for all that I wish you could be
Just let me love, just one last time before I die"

When he finished speaking, his words quavering slightly on practically every syllable, he held his breath till he felt that he must have looked like a smurf underwater. He waited excruciatingly for a response from Ashley.

At first she just sat there stunned in utter silence. Then, she slowly slid her hand across the table and placed it on Connor's hand. "That was a really sweet poem. I really liked it Connor."

A huge sigh of relief flowed out of him, as her touch sent shock waves of electricity coursing through his body, jumpstarting his heart. "You really liked it?" Connor said, making sure he didn't dream her words.

"Yeah, no one's every written anything like that before about me," she said blushing.

Connor couldn't believe that no one had. He'd only known her a few days and he had already written so much about her: her eyes, her voice, her hair, her vulnerability, her lips, her passion, her fury and fear; it seemed there wasn't a topic on her he hadn't touched upon, which by no means did this mean he would stop. "I don't believe that," he said casually.

"Have you been in the solitary confinement room?"

"Uh, no, I haven't had a chance," he said stupidly.

"We should go in there," she said deviously.

Connors blood started to rush like roaring rapids through his veins. "I don't know if we—"

"Don't worry," she cut him off quickly, "you go in there, and I'll sneak in 10 minutes later when the coast is clear."

Connor could think of hundreds of thousands of reasons why this was a terrible idea, but as Ashley glared at him like a ravenous animal about to embark on a feeding frenzy, the thought of them actually being alone, unwatched, was enough to momentarily unplug the rational part of his mind.

"Okay, I hope you know what you're doing, Ash."

Moments later he opened the door to the solitary confinement room, and slipped inside. He was surprised by how dark it was in there. The only light that came in was through the small square window in the door. In the corner of the room there was a mattress. He sat down on the corner of it and waited nervously. Some time passed, and soon the door opened up, and Ashley entered. He laid down letting the anxiousness drain out of him. Ashley bounded towards him with a huge grin on her face, and jumped on top of him.

"This is so wrong yet it feels so right," Connor said as he wrapped his arms around her skinny frame.

"See, I told you I know what I'm doing!" Ashley said as they rolled around on the mattress. They started to play wrestle, giddily like children, almost completely forgetting that just around the corner were several men in white coats. After this exertion they laid side by side staring into each other's eyes. Connor found himself getting lost in the universe that secretly inhabited Ashley's eyes.

"Where have you been all my life?" he asked rhetorically

"Hiding," she said in response.

"You're beautiful," he said almost in a whisper, as an invisible force started to pull them together. Their lips met and time froze; for a fleeting moment the earth ceased to spin on its axis while planes hung suspended in the air like they were a part of a sleeping baby's mobile.

Their lips parted slowly and they both smiled extravagantly.

They turned onto their backs, held each other's hand and cherished their corner of the world in the solitary confinement room.

Before they judged it time to leave, Connor made sure to get Ashley's number so that when they finally got out of this place she couldn't go back into hiding.

She stepped out of the room. Connor waited a little bit and then stepped out of the room as well. Out of the corner of his eye he noticed a man in a white coat eyeing him as he distanced himself from the room. He started to hurry towards the activity room, where he saw Ashley sitting at one of the tables. He was halfway there, right in front of the nurses' station when he felt a finger tap his shoulder and a cold "Excuse me!" emanate from behind him. Connor turned around slowly and was staring into a scrunched disappointed face. "Excuse me! I saw you come out of the room with that woman. I think you know we have rules about that here." "Uh, um," Connor said nervously. "We have a strict no-contact policy, and I've noticed you and that woman becoming quite chummy. You should especially be aware that only 1 person is allowed in the solitary confinement room," the doctor spewed his words like gobs of spit into Connor's face. "W-We-We weren't doing anything wrong," Connor stammered. "You certainly were!" the doctor countered quickly and defiantly. "I can see that the two of you have gotten too close and I forbid the both of you from seeing one another." "You can't do this," Connor said wanting to smash the doctor's face right into the counter of the nurses' station till he was gushing blood all over their files and computers. "You only brought this upon yourself. I'm going to inform the nurses that you are not to go near that young lady. Now please go to your room," the doctor said placing a placating hand on Connor's right shoulder. "Don't fucking touch me," Connor said using all his might to restrain his fist from slamming squarely into the doctor's nose. As if the doctor was hard of hearing he raised his hand back onto Connor's shoulder saying in a soothing voice, "C'mon now, take it easy." Connor shoved the doctor backwards and started sprinting towards Ashley. He reached the table she was sitting at and screamed "They're trying to separate us! They're going to take you away from me!"

"I'm so sorry," she said softly as two orderlies grabbed Connor from behind. "No! Ash, do something!" Connor screamed as he struggled with the two men, rocking back and forth, knocking chairs over and making a tremendous scene. People all around the psych ward were looking at him like he was truly insane, like he truly belonged, as he screamed obscenities at the top of his lungs while he was dragged all the way back to his room.

They closed the door on him resolutely. He pounded his fists on the door for at least an hour till his hands were throbbing and red. His mind started racing wildly. He thought of the stoic look on Ashley's face as they dragged him away kicking and screaming. He thought he might have seen her shaking her head, almost in disappointment, and this thought was too much to bear. It made his heart hurt and shrink. He thought about the possibility of drowning himself in the shower. He thought it would display a twisted sort of justice as the doctors realized they had sent him to his own death, as they dragged his soaking corpse from the bathroom. He thought, and thought, and thought, as he walked towards the bathroom.

He wasn't sure how long he was in the shower before he heard the door open. He got up, his clothes dripping an ocean of water as he walked towards the open door. He stopped under the door frame and yelled furiously, "You can't keep me here any longer! I don't deserve this! None of us deserve this! You're supposed to be here to make us better, but you're not. You make it worse. This place, this vile institution is worse than a jail cell. At least there, you know when you're getting out. You know that that's as bad as it gets. But this place," he paused and lowered his voice for a moment. "In this place, everyday it gets worse!" Then a forceful wave of indignation flowed through his body and there was no way to squelch the oncoming explosion that was about to erupt from within. "You fuckers aren't making anything better," he yelled as he took a few steps forward out of his designated room. "You keep on forcing me to take these drugs, these despicable pills, thinking you know what's wrong with me. Thinking with your big fat brains how fucked up I really am, and in reality, you doctors with your fancy degrees don't really know shit! You've taken the one thing I truly needed and left me with nothing." As he continued to shout obscenities about injustice and cruel and unusual treatment, something caught the corner of his eye. In the hallway outside his room he noticed a painting in a glass frame hanging on the wall. He more than noticed it. It was as if it had punched him excruciatingly in the gut. In this painting there was a sail boat careening through the ocean with a beautiful tri-colored sunset. Instead of filling him with serenity as was surely the purpose, it just made him angrier. A rage that made his blood boil, made him lose whatever control he still had, which suffice to say was not very much at all. He lunged for the painting, water flying from his clothes like a sprinkler gone berserk, as orderlies approached him. Before they could apprehend him he had already torn the painting off the wall, and in an act of desperation Connor chucked it at the floor before the orderlies. It shattered into pieces. Connor thought that that's what had happened to his very own heart. Someone had torn it out and thrown it to the floor shattering it beyond repair, and nobody cared. Two large orderlies grabbed Connor by his arms, as a third orderly slipped on the puddle of water below his feet and went sliding right into the wall. For the second time they began dragging him back into his room. There was a look of insurmountable fear in his eyes as he begged: "No! No! Please don't make me go back into the room. I can't go back. Please! No! I won't go . . ." Tears began to trickle down his cheeks as he was set down on his bed. Two nurses came in with syringes that he knew contained ample amounts of Thorazine. He felt a sense of betrayal as they injected the sedative into both his shoulders. *Not again* he thought, as the sting from the needle seemed to resonate throughout his torso. Knowing that fighting was futile, he lay down and watched as the nurses began to strap him to the bed as one big soaking mess. Their eyes were emotionless. No sorrow or remorse invaded their pupils. He closed his eyes and gave into his despair, as the medication began to numb him, draining him of his energy. *Why God? Why?* He thought, before succumbing to a very deep, forced sleep. It didn't surprise him that he got no answer.

When Connor woke up many hours later the straps were still on him, but his clothes were almost dry. He was thankful that Bob was in the room with him. "Hey, Bob, what time is it?"

"It's almost 10. I was just gettin' set for bed"

"Wait, wait, you gotta get someone in here to get these straps off me."

"Oh, boy, did you cause one helluva scene! I don't wanna cause no more trouble."

"Come on man! This is just like the first night they brought me in!" Connor pleaded

"No, this ain't like that," Bob contested.

"Okay, you're right. I'm mad as hell right now, and I want to kill all those bastards out there, but I promise you Bob, as your friend, if you get me some help, I won't cause anymore scenes."

There was a thick silence that permeated between them for a while, before Bob slowly got up and walked out of the room. *Damn it,* Connor thought exasperated.

Soon a nurse came in with Bob tailing behind her. "You going to be calm?" she asked before reaching for any straps. "Remember, you promised!" Bob said matter-a-factly. "As calm as a lake," Connor responded.

After the nurse unstrapped Connor, and exited the room, he started asking Bob what was going on with Ashley. "Not too much" was his reply.

"You know how much I like her, right? Just like the girl you were with before you came here," Connor tried to explain.

A look of fright swept over Bob's face. "Oh, no! You're not going to hurt anyone are you! You promised you wouldn't."

"Calm down, Bob. Now you're the one making a scene," Connor said jokingly. "I just need you to do something for me."

"I'm not going to hurt anyone!" Bob practically yelled.

Connor was started to get frustrated, so he decided to just blurt it all out: "No, no. All I need you to do is be a messenger boy for me. The doctors won't let me hang out with Ashley anymore, so I'm going to be writing some letters to her and you're going to give them to her. I need her more than anyone seems to know, and if the only bridge of communication left is written words, I'm definitely crossing it." Connor was sure that he had lost Bob for sure with this last sentence but he continued anyway, "You see, Bob, if I lose her, I'll be lost forever in this place, and if I can still reach her through you, then I guess there's still hope for me. I just can't let love slip away again. It's all I got left."

"I gotcha Connor, buddy," Bob said excitedly.

A wan smile slowly crept across Connor's face. "Thanks Bob. You're a true friend."

Bob smiled back, and pretty soon they were both sleeping in their respective beds.

For a few days Bob did his duty, getting letters from Connor and delivering them to Ashley and visa-versa. Connor likened him and Ashley to *Romeo and Juliet,* only instead of feuding families keeping them apart it was doctors with dumb policies. He wrote her about how much he missed and longed for her; wrote about all her wondrous features, and the agony of being so close by, at times even seeing her, but not being able to do anything about it or go near her. He condemned the hospital and most everyone in it, but as long as he could write her, he knew he'd be out soon enough, and then they could both truly be happy together.

Then came the fateful day that changed everything. It wound of changing Connor indefinitely. Bob came in agitated, with the same letter that Connor had just given him moments ago. "What happened?" Connor said perplexed. Bob was silent, with a look of confusion deep in his eyes. "I said, what happened?" Connor said louder.

"She's been discharged," Bob said, sounding out the last word very carefully.

That one word carried with it the heavy weight of something horrible and destructive.

No, it can't be, Connor thought. *She didn't even say goodbye. How could she do this?*

15

In a crazed panic, Connor grabbed the number she had given him that day in the solitary confinement room. "Give me a quarter!" Connor shouted, and Bob was happy to comply. He knew everything would be alright if he could just hear her angelic voice. He ran outside his room and sprinted down to the public pay-phone near the nurses' station. A few people yelled at him to stop running but he didn't pay them any attention. He needed to hear her voice before the timer in his heart ticked down to zero and exploded. He grabbed the pay-phone and punched in the numbers, as quick as he could. *Rrrrrrriiiiiinnnng. Rrrrrrriiiiiinnnng. Rrrrrrriiiiiinnnng.* Then he heard the click, and the voice on the other line: "Hello, you've reached Pizza Hut? What can we get you?" Connor's hand went limp along with the rest of his soul, as the phone slowly fell towards the ground, each "hello" resonating softly in the distance. The timer hit zero in his chest, and his scarred, aching heart fell to the floor, turning blacker than the darkest night, as he waited for oblivion to claim him forever, casting aside any sanity that still remained.

ALPHA CENTAURI

I'm alone in the ocean

Alone among hundreds of other invisible creatures waiting in

immoveable silence . . .

I start on the shore

Each wave beckons

Screams my name softly, maliciously

Each wave caresses my skin

Rocks pelt me

A sharp one cuts me deep

Slowly the salt pours into my wounds and my blood pours into the water

My mind shifts gears . . .

From first to reverse

Nostalgia tears at my mind

It rips every docile muscle apart

I remember you

A sparkle from above reminds me of your eyes

Like stars they lit the abyss

the empty void that was my life

I scrutinize the floor with the soles of my feet

Each step I take

1 2 3 4 5 more

The foam tickles my nose

—I'm captivated by the stars

Each one forces my eyelids open and makes my pupils marvel at their glorious splendor

Fireballs in the sky millions of light years away but I reach for them stupidly

and with each step I convince myself that I'm closer

Closer to them than I'll ever be to you—

Take Orion's belt and time me a noose with it

Let the scorpion poison me

I'll walk until I can reach a star

Alpha Centauri greets the black horizon

Ruminate: If I could only hold it in my palm

—I rob it from God ignorantly, and he decides my treacherous destiny

It sears my flesh

The atrocious star causes so much pain

but I grasp it tighter and tighter

till my bones feel the heat

till my marrow boils

Then I offer you my star

And you wish upon it . . .

Never To See Me Again

I bow my head defeated, acceptingly, passively

and continue my march out to sea

Choking on the water

till I can't breath

till fishes swim in my broken lungs

I'll grant you your wish

Vanishing into the vast blue hideously remarkable ocean

Bruised and Condemned by the Heavens

Smothered and Suffocated by the Supernal Sea

but Destroyed by you

WOULD YOU

If you knew how much I needed you
would you pick up the phone when I call

If it made sense for us to be together
would you call us soul mates

When you left without a goodbye
I knew this goodbye would last until eternity

Never leave me again
Never see me again
Never be me again

If my lips craved yours
would you let your teeth sink into me

If your smile is suspended in my brain
would you help me drag it down
                    Destroy it, shattered, jagged pieces of you
                    Leftover in my mind
When you left like an elusive dream
I knew you'd haunt my nightmares

FALL FROM HEAVEN

I have fallen from heaven
into your eyes
into a better heaven
without lakes of fire
filled with beauty and hazel oceans

I have fallen from heaven
into your delicate hands
to a better place
filled with your face
It's a sad case

I could fall from this heaven with you
You know I'd do . . .
Anything, for one kiss that'll send me back
to the heavenly sky

I'm shy and afraid of you
so make it easy
and ask one question while I muse
"Can I use you?"
and I'll reply "Anytime you need"

THIS VENT'S FOREVER BLOWING

You vent
And it's like the world is crumbling down
    On your shoulders
        All around
            These are the stepping stones you walk
    The ones I asked for
        As a child
        As an innocent
      In my bed
      I prayed
      Not to get laid
      Before I knew what that meant
Like a chicken trapped in a cage
One flew over the cuckoo's nest
It's more than prayers heard
        Answered
        Given
        Received
        Listen
      Listen, Listen
        Please . . . .

I had a simple request as I lied
    As I cried
    Just someone to find
After a while I thought it dumb
That He wasn't listening
But with immense ears and beautiful eyes
She heard—

The will is yours
The way is there, up, up, up, up and don't go down

Have faith, like one should
Like an L.A. Story that never got finished

The words he wrote and narrated
"There is someone out there for everyone
even if it takes a pitch axe, night goggles,
and a shovel to find."

So I looked on the ground for her
I looked to the sky
      High
      Shy
      Dry
      My
Ever-lasting peace that's missing
Another war being fought
But without any sacrifice
This battlefield earth is no more
Are you sure?
I pray every night for it
Mother nature creaks and moans
Forgives, Forgets

In the wood that comes from the Earth
It pierced my toe
The devil was kind, was mine
and she took it away
The pain, remorse, with empty eyes
The wood was plucked
And now I look to the sky for her
A star, a galaxy, a milky swirl in the night
Just someone who will be with me
And remind me not to give up this fight
like Shinning night lights I flicked on whenever the shadows swirled
      Find her and begin again, and give birth to life
        Instead of this never-ending strife.

I Love You Utopia

I Before, Now

I was in the darkness although lights shone all around me
I would get lost in it all
The treachery, and pain
I would wallow every day without a choice
Adjusting to it, breaking and bending
                  Falling deeper into a black hole of anguish from
                  which seemed inescapable

Now I'm in a room
Dark as the night
Dark as the way my life use to be
A pitch black room—
That shines gloriously in the brightest way
A pitch black room—
My soul cascading light, breaking the darkness
How did the darkness disintegrate?
What made it disappear?
What has made it beautiful?
Another presence is sensed
Light streaming from their soul, brighter and purer—
Lighting my life
Making it shine
Ah yes, You are there
You are what has made my room gleam
My Life   Perfect

II Goodbye

Backseat:
Kissing the sweetest lips ever created
Feeling the heat pulsate around us—Not bothered
Together we're invincible
Droplets of moisture stick to us like pollen to bees
Together we don't mind

10:30:
Lying in a marvelous way
Arms wrapped around each other
Gazing into eyes dreamily
Thoughts meander through our heads
Hoping to be wrong, glancing at the digits
Sometimes blue, sometimes red, sometimes green
No matter what the color, or image the message projected is always the same
The Time—
We will be torn apart
Time to let go—
Torn apart within minutes
Time to say goodbye—
We will be together again
Time for us to fade to memory—
Memories that will last till the end of Time

You gave me such an officious goodbye
but it was not enough
The hours on the clock run by like they are being chased
I turn away after grasping you one last time
smelling you—feeling your soft cheek against mine
Indignation flows through me as I'm forced to leave you
but I know we will still be together—
I am not scared to say forever
Together Forever.

III The Beauty

Lying so close in each others arms
Sprawling our limbs every which way . . .
Staring into you
Getting trapped in your beautiful, extraordinary eyes
Your Supernal face
Looking at it makes my heart flutter
You are my heavenly dream
My hearts desire
Everything I ever wanted, needed
And I muse about everything I feel
I meander through my soul and spirit in hopes to find something
someway to express the feelings in a simplistic way

Lying next to you
staring into your angelic hazel eyes
I can't even begin to describe the feelings that course through my body every time
Feelings I've never felt before
feelings I will never forget
I love your eyes, the way they catch the light
the way they sparkle
Irises that entrap me
The most magnificent eyes I've ever seen
Could write a novel about your eyes—
I love your face, your soft skin
the cutest freckles
A perfect nose, lips
A true masterpiece, heavenly
A creation of true beauty
The brush, remarkable

If you were to perambulate through my mind
You'd see you

everywhere you scrutinized

every turn you took

Your picture plastered on all sides

Your voice echoing repeatedly

And your face in the center, with those glorious eyes, lighting up everything

Destroying the gloom and shadows that once existed

Thoughts of you engulfing all the evils that were looming, replenishing with exuberant

happiness and feelings long forgotten; never felt

IV Love

You broke through the panoply

healed the scars

revived my soul

and have given me a reason to feel again

to . . . . Love Again

Perhaps that is it

The whirlwind of feelings swimming in my soul

My pulse speeding up—

The butterflies I get when I see you

My heart slamming itself against my ribcage—

The way my mind shuts down and I forget coherent speech when around you

it all spells out the same words

I played this game so many times

Been hurt

been deceived

Felt like a pawn

but now I feel . . . .

Like a king on top of the world!

and you are my queen!

Oh and no cushion large enough could have lessened the impact of this fall

The way I fell for you

You are a savior

You are an angel

a godsend it seems

And I will admit it to myself before I admit it to anyone else

Before I even say it out loud I will write it here for only my eyes to see

I Love you

And I will say it aloud and I will take it to sleep with me

For now it will remain a secret

And when we're ready in our Utopia

In our world where nothing exists except us—where your beauty radiates all around us

Where I am invisible and nothing could possible hurt me

And even if I were to die that moment it wouldn't matter

In our Utopia when I first realized what these feelings were

In our Utopia where your touch and your abundant beauty leaves me speechless and frozen

In this Utopia where you will read this and where I will tell you

I Love You

I truly do

A Star So Close I Can Touch

If you took away my sunshine
would I still want to make you mine
somewhere over the rainbow and out to sea
on the sandy beaches, carefree

If you took away my dark
would I want you to stay with me
forever ever like in all those love songs
Sincere as can be

They play in my head endlessly
Like you're my record out of tune, or wordless
Awkward and befuddled
Just got to be cuddled

It's ringing in my head
the way I felt dead
Before
Sore to the core, crying forevermore

I felt sorry
I felt bad
Loathsome and Lonesome, Longsome Lycanthrope
I'm a loner
And all I want
All I wish
As she wishes
Is to be alone

Alone next to the star burning bright in the sky
Always reminding me of you
On the cloudless beaches in Valencia
Of the b-b-q'ed woody fragrance
that couldn't compare to the clean
laundry
in your basement

On a recliner fit for a foolish fucking king,
But I didn't act like the right one
So I lost it to oblivion-

Ursa Major, bring me down to Earth
Destroy this black hole in me
Because you're the closest star I see . . . .

DON'T GO WHEN I FALL

When I fall 2,000 feet
Into the core of our world
Who will save me?
Will she wrap her panoply of fire around me
Keep me safe, like snoopy on a blanket
or singe my soul
What color will it turn
Hopefully still fluorescent and annoying

If no one saves me
Will God send a cloud down
Miles of clouds to bring us up
or do I not deserve this victory
or should my life be ancient history
His story . . . .

When is my ending coming
Is it around the corner
Vicious men with guns,
Waiting to blow me into smithereens
Release my soul
Oh, how clean-
It can be
Because even when I shut my eyes
I still can see-
This little bit of hope clings to me
Don't go away from me

BENEATH THE EARTH

Are you the one?

Will it ever be done?

Am I the chosen one?

All these questions that should have answers

But there's a mess I've created in my brain

It complicates what shouldn't be complicated

Maybe those 21 grams no longer exist

Maybe I'm just a demon on wheels ready to crash

Ready for this opaque oblivion to bring me to them

Bring me straight down with an elevator

Or shoot me like a star out of a cannon straight into heaven

Are the points even?

Am I trying my hardest anymore

No, because I say fuck the score

6-9 could be 9-6

They're numbers that haunt me

Follow me around every corner

Numbers waiting to beat my face with a crow bar

I would deserve it

Because I didn't mark her face when I slammed my white knuckle across her paper face

Because my sin wasn't revealed back to me in her black eye

The evil that men do . . . I have done it

and it is unforgiving and I cannot rest

I won't pass this test

I would like to buy a crest

Hang it around someone else's neck

Someone I've never known yet she saw me cry many times

Not the one who saw it in person

Rather, something, someone different
Who never got a chance to know me
Who was mean at first, then showed me pictures of a beautiful beach
No, the beach wasn't beautiful.
Only she was . . . .

The past lingers
The sentiment of I do's
and don'ts

I wrote a book about her beauty
And will I ever get over the fact that I gave it all up for her once
In my mind I thought it was time
and I told her severely "I cannot be your friend"
Because I never was
I was a boy in love
A pathetic boy and his prick out of control
An addiction I welcome with open arms
But whose arms will cradle me when I'm dying
The same girl as always, my guardian angel
No. Though she needs me, Though I probably need her
Something else I need . . . .

Someone else always in the background
In the dark crevices of my heart
I kept her memory dry
Cleaner than clean, completely unseen
By her I wish to be seen
and get dirty in the soil beneath us
Get lost in the volcano about to erupt in my heart
Let the lava turn us into magma so no one can find us
because we will be beneath the earth

"Get It" Or A Short Lesson On Alliteration

We'll get through this together
This distorted synapses sparking
Psychotically
And I can't stop or control
this burning in my mind

Give me time
To remember,
I'm still alive
Dismember
Saw through electricity

Dire Disturbances Drawing my blood
Give me the needle
Right through the eyes
and take whatever you need

Who even placed the seed?
Was it the devil or something deeper
Some creeper with peepers
empty unaccomplished eyes praying for pain

I feel such disdain
while I'm trying to heal through the eyes of a stranger on the brink
but it's not working
no it's not working

Flailing failing fumbling frantic fanatic
what can I do but succumb to the noise

I have no choice
I have only one voice

It's the one that floats through the air
exalted and sincere, slightly saccharine
Unlike the traitors reaching for blades
to cut down this scar across my chest

A reverse operation
Don't forget to put in a new one
It could be my redemption
Just give me a new one before I awaken

You could say my vitals are deceased
You could say I really have the disease
You could say I'm neurotic
You could say my face looks tragic
You could say I had to loose it
Just to figure out how to get it

Get it?

(I'll never sport claws of damnation
Desperate for some kind of celebration
even as my life hits an all time low
I'll pretend it's apart of the show)

But what do I know?

THE FIRST TIME

These tears they scold my cheeks and cut them open

My face bleeds, like for the first time

Perhaps it always feels like the first time

My heart being crushed is becoming so mundane

But it hurts . . . .

This time I can't pick my disgusting heart back up off the floor

This time I can't piece together the ventricles

But I try . . . .

I try anyway to pick it up but the jagged edges cut my fingers

My fingers bleed like it's the first time

It always feels like the first time

But I cry . . . .

And one day hope that I may die and not feel this pain

This anger . . . . this vindictive cold feeling . . . I'm not use to it . . . .

I love you Utopia

I loved you unconditionally

I loved it when you smiled so bright it lit up my life

I loved it when you'd bury your head in my chest because you were blushing so radiantly

I loved it when you did everything that you did

All the idiosyncrasies . . . . all the faults

You were perfect in my eyes

Perfection

You were my heaven

But something changed in you

Something turned black and chose not to cherish me

I always cherished you

Something became rotten and chose not to hold me anymore

I never wanted to stop holding you

And that was the problem wasn't it . . . .

I hate you Utopia

I fall to the ground my knees scraping against my shattered heart

Blood leaks out of them . . . .

It hurts . . . .

I'm lying in my own unconditional blood

You cut me open . . . .

Blood floods my eyes and stings them

It's like the first time . . . .

Please God, let this be the last time.

EDGE OF OUR WORLDS

I'm drowning in the opaque waters
As I am so very fond of doing
It's ethereal, surreal, unreal
And yet this habitual suffocation doesn't have me frightened
As I am sure I probably should be
My last breath is on its way
because you took it from my uncompromising lips

Will you be capable of dragging me out of the dirty waters of solitude and sadness
This whirlpool, I feel it sucking me down
Pulling, Pulling
Also uncompromising, but for different reasons, malicious motives-
Killing and Killing
Do I feel like dying again?
Do the whole thing over?
(Encore!)
Truly choke on these magnificent bubbles in the water
If I wake up to her
I'll be the victim
Because the 1st time was done all wrong
There was no song to sing
And she'd be gone, gone
She wouldn't be wrapped in my weak embrace
I would not have been so somber, solemn, sideways
So cynical
Hateful
A fist full of rage but no vent forever blowing
No outlet

An ocean of anger flowing magically around me, suspended and red as fire

And I can't make it stop

I am the submissive one, the prisoner, the one going gleefully toward the trap

Like an imbecile

Like a genius with no brain

It would have all been irrelevant

Had I woken up to a pair of brown eyes, a glow like nightlights

Like mine but better

May they forgive me

My harsh words

My quivering hands

Everything done wrong

Let this redundancy play

Vacant eyes of blue led me astray

and this is no epopee

Nor do I seem capable of creating one

Not in this ephemeral moment

But still this is a silent cry for her, the muse

Before I leave everything behind

Like this knife in my side

Like the damages to my pride

The way everything makes me want to run and hide

Will you be the exception?

Can you be my salvation?

Fix my broken wings

Make the hurt cease

Do something at least . . . .

I know I'll run from you as if I were being chased

Facilitate this connection, and walk after me

For I adore your face

even as my vision blurs

I can picture it in the water, through the blackness, through the darkness behind these

closed lids

Beyond beautiful . . . .

With all my might and will I'll reach my hand up over the edge of the ocean above

Give me your hand and let us stay by the edge, the coast so enchanted

Like those pictures you showed me by the sand

I haven't forgotten

and I know I may fall off the edge without you, or my lungs may fill with water

so take my docile hand before it's too late

and catch me as I fall off the edge of our worlds . . . .

This dreadful suicide wasn't wise

but it's fine

because I can see infinity in your eyes

WISH I COULD DRAW

If I were an artist
and my brush was clean
I would paint you the grandest portrait
anyone has ever seen

I would use purple pastels
and a golden frame that
matches your eyes

There is no red that can match your cheeks or you hair
and nothing could truly capture the beauty in your pupils
Though I'd try uselessly, endlessly

I'd try with my shaky hands
and hope that I don't fail
because it would mean everything to me
if you could see it

And I would never hang it on a rusty nail
I would cherish the canvas always
every inch of it
Hide it away from all the horrors in this world

Protect it from myself
Keep it in my heart
There's room between the scars—

You are the epitome of beauty
nothing I could draw would do you justice
wish it could be just us
marvelous and serene
Like a dream I haven't seen

* * * * * * * * * * * * * * * * * *

After it's all said and done
and the sunset in the painting
doesn't match the one in the sky
I'll surrender
Put my hands up and confess
Yes!
The real sunset reminds me of you
isn't as beautiful as you
And if I were blinded by the sun
Squinting at it as I do
I'd still see you in my mind's eye
Through closed lids and damaged visions
because I already see you everywhere

MIRACLES

A love like I've never known
And they say that knowledge is power
so without you I'm weak
A fierce disingenuous lady would call me some disgraceful name
And she should be the one covered from head to toe in shame
You can sense the sticky stench she left behind
It comes at me from all sides
but when you're near
I'm sure I will have nothing to fear
except my own mind and it's terrible tangents soaked with doomed deceptions
and my purpose to see your soul, or merely touch you hand
You may be the one in command
I'll be like a doll you play with
but content and complacent,
with real limbs and a beating heart
Like a place I've been sent-

Heaven: like a love I've never known
And they are dark
Each pupil like a black hole in the wondrous cosmos
I use to fear the darkness and shadows
but now I travel through it like a wounded soldier
feeling the blood quicken,
the adrenaline rushing through my veins
prepared for death
like a man that shouldn't be alive
I'll dive
Straight into them carelessly
Fearlessly
because what have I got to loose besides you
Like loosing heaven again

Not even God would wish that upon me

A son among glorious sons

I prayed for a soul-mate under the covers as a small child,

in desperation and despair

in quiet subtle whispers in an empty hopeless room

Has he finally heard?

And there are signs leading me to you

Call it a portrait, Call it a gut-wrenching feeling, Call it the real thing

Call it the tears that stream down my face because I haven't seen you enough

Face to Beautiful Face

And the last time, the wicked witch condemned me in a place of wonderment

A place I snuck into whenever I wanted to

Dreams on Screens

But I couldn't talk to you, even though I couldn't peel my eyes away

So I'm still that boy praying, delaying

Saying: "Remember me?"

I'm right where I always been

As my name becomes synonymous with sin

Will I be alright on that night

Can I save myself from the echoing din

The fake voice may grow hoarse and fade away forever

As you may be the miracle with no divine intervention needed

Because your creation is miracle enough

HATE TO SEE

I know what it's like to feel the world crumbling
To see it all come down on me, crushing me pass suffocation
Watch every hideous ash pass before my hazy eyes
Dilated, glassy dead eyes filled with daggers of fury
Wish someone would reach in and grab them
Stab me, blind me, detest me-
Shove them deep in my irises
So I can't get lost in the blue ocean of your eyes-
Was it just a part of my own fate
To make me stronger as I fall faster, further
Another love that turns angry

This pain will never end
It'll only obliterate something beautiful
Something that I was never meant to see
Sending everything into oblivion
Like the emptiness I feel in my soul
It's an empty hole full of discarded memories
I don't need them because I've lost the will to survive
And I thought I had a spark
Ready to ignite this world
But here I stand with an empty gasoline container
though nothing need catch flame in order for me to burn

If you searched my brain

Perambulated each sickly dark corridor that was filled with pictures of you

Images that made me feel normal, that lit up my mind, something glorious

Now they must be torn down

Savagely, Insanely

In a justifiable rage

This prison, this cage

Scrutinize the trash on the floor and you'll know

Love has been lost

and it's leaking like blood from my ears

because I know you'll never be here

Too much to bear, stare, care

In love and war, it's all fair

Just leave me on the floor weeping

Till my eyes are so dry, I see sand

And I feel my veins giving up on me

Till there's nothing left of me

But this hate that everyone can see

I CAN'T

You could shred my heart
and watch each shard
fall to the floor

You could take my brain
make it insane
and left for someone else

You could take my limbs
on a whim
and beat me with them

You could break my bones
break them with sharp stones
and leave me aching, shaking

because I'm already there
My heart stopped beating long ago
for a second that has never stopped ticking

My brains out of control
spinning and winding
meandering and stalling

My limbs are weak
not capable of moving me
towards anything of true meaning (like the ceiling)

My bones hold up skin
pale, and horrid
I am a blank canvas without the beauty

You could give me a muse
and pry my eyes open
because they're closed

Nostalgia like the devil bringing me back
and I can't remember the good times
all I remember . . . . is all I remember
and it still hurts

Apathy eating at me everyday that you're not here
lack of empathy overwhelming me, crushing me
That fucking needle dripping neurosis
and in my veins there's always poison

You could call me addicted
You could say I'm afflicted
You could say I'm being haunted
because all I want
all I need-

What I don't have is the inner peace
or the pieces of the puzzle that were never meant to be put together
Dismantle me and make it work
For God's sake make it work
because this is killing me

You could calm my fears
You could salvage those tears
You could stay away
You could stay forever
You could create a paradox
with or without you
You could cause a conundrum
in this vicious cycle of treachery
You could agonize over this
You could, You could

I wish I could
but I can't

GOODBYE

I remember you and me

So happy on the outside

Our faces smiling, our eyes gleaming

on the inside

our souls dark, our minds depressed, and our hearts worn

I'd stare through the transparent sadness, right at you

right into you beautiful brown eyes

where I would get lost

lost forever and ever surrounded by love and hope

in a world where nothing else mattered because we had each other

where we could not be hurt

where we were invincible to the monster we all fear

the monster which can kill us all in the end: pain

and yet, within this magnificent world filled with flowers, and pink clouds

the monster lurks, watching, waiting for his next victim

that victim which is you

and me destined to be your savior

but I failed

too ignorant to see your sorrow

too scared to accept the truth

and now as I sit here pondering what exactly happened

trying to put together the twisted puzzle that taunts me every night and everyday

I think back to the day when the world full of love and pure happiness broke into a
thousand pieces

I now look upon my world filled with dread and pity

where hate and loneliness reign supreme power

my soul weeps day and night in this dark world, alone

on my own

I often think back on the better days

days when I would hold your hand

our hearts beating in sync

and we would lie next to each other, and I would hold you wishing time would stop and I

could hold you for eternity

your laughter sounding like the most beautiful symphony I ever heard

your face radiating your beauty

our minds connected

our souls free and pure

but now I see your face, knowing that when you see me your eyes fill with hate

and I hear your laughter, and pain ricochets through my body

through my spine, through my mind, and into my eyes

my cold eyes forced to look upon a loveless world from which there is no escape, full of

dead ends, and nowhere roads

my eyes shed tears of pain and frustration

I know that I have no one to blame

I can only blame myself

my selfish acts have left me miserable and defeated

my heart is worn

my legs tremble beneath me

and my soul has stopped mourning and it has left me dead to the world

because now

I know it is over

there is nothing more I can do

so I put away my love and bury it deep beneath these ventricles

and say goodbye to it

and in turn I say goodbye to you

No One Knows

Carve out my eyes with your knives
take my heart and smash it against the wall
kill someone in a stall

No one knows how I feel
always alone

Destroy all the puppies
Smear their brains on the concrete
Diagnosis: Self Induced Psychosis
So stay away before the pressure makes me explode

No one knows how I feel
always dead on the inside

On the outside flames sear my flesh
Jump into an ocean of hate
There's no such thing as fate

Massacre you enemies
Tear out the guts of your nemesis

No one knows how I feel
in my broken heart

An Easy Formula

Thinking of hurting yourself

Call 679-1112

We'll hang up!

Free, anonymous, confidential

Don't tell the parents!

Who's running away

Who's slitting their wrists in the dark shadows

flirting with death—becoming charmed

Stale air—Carbon Monoxide

It'll Kill

I can live, I can die in this

Loveless world

Picking, Picking at the walls

Depression is anger turned inward

Sadness is temporary

Why would someone cut themselves

It's a release

Cooking is a wonderful therapy

Says an obese man in the cascading light

Drugs, Drugs, Drugs

Pumping through our cut veins

Tear us open

Crank Acid Spitting Fucks

That's us

We are the dead

The doomed generation

1 in 5 teens attempt suicide

girls attempt, boys succeed

Succeed in dying

Their testosterone bragging

Bam!   Brains Splattered

Bullet smile ear to ear

When a person sticks the shaft of a gun in their mouth and pulls the trigger and no cne's

around

Does it make a sound?

Does it float through the air

Does it fluctuate

Do you understand

Distraught?

Bewildered?

You're not exempt

The fingers are pointing at you

You!

They're digging into your eyes deep deep

You're the reason they're dying

Okay, Fine

Here's an easy formula they gave me with a knife, two blue capsules and a noose

perfectly fitted for my neck

Loss + Isolation = depression = suicide

Apparently we're all suicidal

Don't keep it a secret

Even in your subtle whispers

Don't be apart of the doomed generation

Just be a volunteer for the dead

ACTION

Action
A word that comes like a knife
Act
Say the words you say
Say the words you don't say
Say the words you can't say
Killllllllllllllllllllllllllllllll
Or don't say a word
Lock it like a prison
So that no one escapes
or just Act

Action
Keep it all together
Keep it all right
Keep it for the night
Dreammmmmmmmmm
But don't say a word
And don't act it out
Don't shout, or pout
doubt—
Pain in the rain that comes from your sparkling essence
Give it up, Give in, Give up?
Shame like a thousand cratered moons that remind me of you some how
Like the dark eyes I see through
With wet fingers and solemn feet
Create it
Shake it
Try not to fake it
Because it feels like the first time, every goddamn last time
Hannnnnnnnnnnnnnnnnnd

Give me your hand
Because I knew you before I knew myself
And it'll echo forever beneath my flesh
The beat's never ending
And you probably never really heard it
Losttttttttttttttttttttttttttttttt
On the cross
Everyday, not looking either way
Just walking with eyes closed
Thoughts, up and away
But where is Today
And when did we forget
This never-ending regret

. . . .

Torn like a flower, like leaves between my hands. Gentle and delicate, forever broken.
Forever bruised. Forever stuck on pause, flitching for the future forever forgetting fine
days. Crying days. Lying days. Flying days. Trying days . . . .

Torn like the roots from the bulldozer, yellow and mean. No one knows what it has seen.
Definitely not something pristine, clean. Dirty and ugly, like the dirt from shoes. But do
you have anything to lose . . . .

Action like the bodies in the streets
Killed with the guns from those terrible tanks
Dream because you know not how to live
Hand me something before I get
Lost.

BURY ME

I'm sinking deeper within
Into this dark cold oblivion
No one can save me now
Not you, not me, or her eyes
I'm drowning in the numbness that's eating away at my soul
I'm alone, truly alone
I'm invisible
Eyes see through me . . . .
No, they see nothing
I am less than air
No one breathes me, no one needs me
No one dares touch me because I am a disease
I am the pestilence that will invade you the first chance I get
I will love you like a parasite
I will smother you till I die
I'll seek you out till you Kill me
Cure yourself of my rotten and decrepit touch
Then I will return to complete and utter nothingness
It's where I belong

Give me metal, put me behind bars

Give me a lock, throw me behind bars

Deny me hinges, don't let me out of this cell

But don't ever give me hope, or love ever again

Shut me out from the world

Send me away, force me into solitude

Shoot me out into space letting the fires turn my cheeks to ash

Smoldering my bones, melting my heart

But please, don't show me happiness

It's more than I can take . . . .

Build me a vault for all my dead and dying memories

Bury me beneath the Joy, beneath the heartbreak, beneath the exaltation

beneath the love, and beneath the beginning

Bury me so deep I won't be able to see or breath or hear or feel at all

Bury Me, because I'm already dead

Fire Within

I welcome this catharsis
I embrace this muse
I long for your kiss
I have nothing to lose

The sparkle in your eyes
is sometimes too bright
even under this lazy light
What a sight!

Suffocation as a daily ritual
Drowning to learn to breath
Dying just to live
Burning just for fun

These freckles where I wish to reside
The red nails that carve into my hide
remind me of the pain in pleasure
All of this is beyond measure

A love that unfurls
as we start to dissolve
A smile that curls
as I start to unravel

You are the sutures that make amends
You are the white in black and white
You are the fantasy within reality
You are the surreal that's more than real

This recycled air makes me dizzy
Exhale, breathe in, learning to breathe once again
Letting my guard down again
Allow this to begin

This is the truth that is deception
The thoughts not worth thinking
Like the glorious
Rejection of Perception

You are the wonders that never cease
You are the puzzle that's missing a piece
A love that can never be released

The grass growing beneath my feet, you are
The grey-blue in the sky that comes from your eyes
While the clouds shade your beauty
and the rain drops caress your skin
You spark the fire within

Subconscious Suicide

Taking imprudent steps I glide off the platform from which I stand
Committing Suicide in a sense
I crash through boards of my subconscious
Marvelous things flow around me
mixed in with treachery and depression
Images of hated faces I buried beneath
Feelings of jealousy cascade through my eyes
Even the one I loved is there, still there waiting to hurt me
I see edentulous smiles from the big screen
Hopes for an epopee are disappearing
With these and more I forget my supernal thoughts of her
and I bury them within this void of consciousness
Locked away never to be opened
I walk down this corridor pleasantly wrapped in my shield of lies
No more thoughts to keep me down
I take one last look at my memories from before
and I hope never to commit suicide again

SUBCONSCIOUS SUICIDE

THE WAY

I won't let you fall
If I have to carry all these ugly demons on my back forever
If I have to stall before I crawl
Before I speed up and slip

Though I know that's just you in my heart
shaking furiously along with my insane thoughts
but these thoughts are just inane
With me since birth

Re-birth
You know

I'm afraid
As afraid as I was
Quavering, quivering before the quixotic queen
Quite quiet, I'll be
Afraid of the words that could shatter the night sky into shards or telescopes reflecting
stars
And they would only fall onto the glorious pavement magnifying your profound
elegance
Show it to me

Key, Key, Key
Not what it use to be
Just snake eyes wanting to stare into yours
And get lost, lost, lost and then the adventure can begin
I'll close my eyes and we can rise together

Above the atmosphere I'll be your guide
Or below the ground I'll face them
I won't back down
If I have to take these arms and hold it all up
Like a psychotic sphere swirling in my stomach

But I know what's right and the path less taken, the wrong ways
And I've taken it everyday
And when I was just an innocent in those hallways
I took it to you

The hardest path that led me towards the grandest journey with gleaming scarecrows
and white doves soaring, regrets and bones, alone, and in the basement with the
blackest lights
She had me
but clear your worried mind

because it's a photograph, like a sign, bent in the middle, with scribbles on the other side
and it's what I've done
what I couldn't stop
because once this explosive struck my soul
I could only see your red strands, even after a fire scorched a highway
This, is the high way

The right way?
The wrong way?
The only way to you-
Don't go away with the rest of them

MARIA

Maria you got to help me
get out of this household
get out of this skin that's been infected by fury

Maria you got to break me
and take me home
and shake my hand till it falls to the floor

Maria you got to meet her
because she'll change your life

Maria you got to forsake me
get out of these shoes
get out of this life made to lose

Maria you must take me
to a place where the rainbows cover your eyes
and the face you see is more than heavenly

Because I love you

One Experiment

My life's an experiment gone haywire
    throw me into the fire
    and let the news be dire

Cry for a bit
Take a hit
Throw a fit

My life's a never ending experiment
    and every day I vent
when pen glides across the page
    and all you want's revenge

Fragile, docile boy missing everything
    Kissing everyone
because personal contacts a must-see
    Be me, it's harder than they know
    My foes stab me daily
They come from the future with weapons to hurt me

but I feel no pain
and my neck's a crane
climb up it and jump in my mouth

My life's an experiment gone completely wrong

FILL ME

Dear Mother
did you ever think I'd end up like this
with a crying fist
and one dying wish

Dear father
did you ever think I'd be such a bother
with a loving hole
and a falling sun

Move me, Consume me, Thrill me, Chill me, Kill me, Fill me

Dear son
did you ever think it'd be easy
with a knife in your hand
and a half colored moon

Dear Sister
did you think you'd succumb
to all the madness in one
times like these never end

Move me, Consume me, Thrill me, Chill me, Kill me, Fill me

YOU LOOKED STONED

You looked stoned
and moved in slow motion
and shoved a rice krispie in your mouth
Nothing behind those eyes
The ones filled with dark green flowers
and a crazy streak
Within me you're gone
Within me I'm gone
Within me . . .
Within me . . .
Bleeding over me
An excitement like no other
A sick and twisted game that broke my face
Couldn't believe what I saw
Like smoke that consumes me
I choke and suffocate on you for the last time

THE MAGICIAN AND THE QUEEN

You could be my heroin
You could be the substance coursing through my veins
and then none of this would have been in vain
and even though my heart can't forget the rain
and what's left behind was an evil stain
You could be my heart
Unbroken
Unscarred
Undamaged
Untouched
like it's never been
Can't erase the thing's I've seen
or will see
But see me for who I am
Not the horror within my bones, not the traitor
In the marrow

Want to feel you in my cells
Want to make room for you in the center
Where you will always feel safe
Where there's no danger
Where you will be beautiful forever
Because to me you always will be
Always were

This blood so intense, pumping
Augmenting each revelation that comes streaking across these dumbstruck eyes
Like lost spirits I gathered
Like images from another life
Showing me the path in this one
I'd walk it with no legs for you

I'd drag myself with my teeth

Because I've never desired something more

which leaves me with this undeniable fear

so relentless

May my redemption come

while I burn in the sweet fire you provide

And if this isn't mutual

Leave me

Let me lay charred and defeated

There's no need for a burial-

I've already been buried

Suffocated and beaten

By other demons

But if you lay me down

At least I'd have touched your essence for a fleeting moment

That is my heaven

Much like the irises that have me captured

You have captivated me in future screens and scenes

And these words I write for you

Will never cease

Because our love could be endless

Beyond the eternity that lies in the palm of your hand

May I clasp it?

The Magician and the Queen dinning without a care in this world or the next

Breathing Breathless Before you . . .

YOUR TEETH

What I would do to get to you
Hell isn't an obstacle
I'd let the fire burn my Holy feet
Let the tiny demons poke me with their cute pitchforks
Was your face the one I saw before my eyes
Closed forevermore
Did your red lips wake me
They certainly shake me
Even when your face has a guise
A black mask to hide the rest of your beauty
I still have an untouched package for you
A present I hope you will enjoy

It's your teeth
Never would I break them
Because your smile, ear to precious ear
Is what I long for
I saw you by the shore
Some pictures etched in my mind
Didn't realize they would ever mean so much
Or that I'd catch you as chemicals
drained from my brain
Put a gun to my head if you think me insane
But it only pulls the trigger for you
I only need you to catch my tears
and quiet the evil within
All my meaningless sins
Made meaningful for you

I want to be the sand between your toes

The rays that make you sun burnt

The water that keeps you fresh

The rock wall you climb

And if the sun explodes

as I drown in your waters

Keep climbing the mountain

Don't ever fall

I'll take the biggest fall for you

because I fell for you before

And I didn't stop my feet from walking away

Like traitors to the cause

Like ambivalent ruminations in my head

I want you to sleep safely in my bed

And I'll wake you with my black eyes

Just to make you smile once more

It may be all I need . . .

Drop a seed-

And let the tree spin round us

MY DREAMS AND MY NIGHTMARES

Like cancer
You kill me
Like darkness
You take me

Forever you invade
my dreams and my nightmares

Like hate
You fill me
Like love
You destroy me

Forever you invade
my dreams and my nightmares

Like the clouds outside my window
You rain on my parade
Like the storm in my mind
You change my nerves

Like a knife jetting across a crowded room
Like your eyes
Like a bomb that blows my mind
I love you like a queen

GOD HELP US

I killed our savior
There was no one to save Him
I watched as they sat him down
and whipped Him
I could hear the sound of each sharp strand piercing his back
The skin fell like ribbons
Blood formed a lake on the ground
Pontius exclaimed with glee: let the torture begin!
Our savior would look to Pontius and see a twisted grin
In His blood we see no reflection
Can't we see the damage we inflict everyday
Still waiting for his resurrection
Is there another way-

Time for the nails
I drill one into his wrist
the pain in his face
in pure bliss
The solace of achieving this rite
is beyond measure
No remorse is felt as the blood leaks through the splinters
Another by his feet
and it's my fault
it's everyone's fault
All eyes soak in the torment
as I place this crown of thorns upon His head
wondering when he will be dead

Yes, let the trepidation sink in

Show me your fear

let the darkness consume you

let the hate rape you till there is nothing left

let this atrocity destroy your very soul if you even have one

but no-

barely anything is perceived

It is the hardest thing to conceive

In his eyes

fading and fluttering as he slowly dies

There isn't contempt

He does not despise us

There isn't confusion

He does not feel betrayed

In his eyes, glorious and wide

we see sorrow laced with hope

and it shines so bright that even among the treachery and corruption

the dark in all our souls is obliterated

and there is nothing left to do but wait for the reckoning

swift and formidable as it may be

God help us

I Am Still in the Dirt

I was wrong when I said we couldn't be buried

You can't be buried with your unfathomable will

but here I am still

In the dirt

I can feel it in my teeth

the sick grime

and All I wanted to do was make you mine

but you closed the coffin tight as can be

With eyes closed so you couldn't see

You buried me below everything that's ever mattered

This sentimentality is killing me, I think as my breath starts to run out

and without a doubt

I know if your hand reached down for me I'd be okay

but no way

Your white hand, with piercing red nails could destroy anything that got in its path

but I am not on your road no longer

like a sick sick detour into an elaborate hell

Etched in my mind are those eyes which brought with them: simply heaven

So I wallow

and I flail

and I curse the Gods for abandoning me

not hearing my prayers, on soft ears they linger still

I reminisce of the curve, one last visual

or the beautiful reddish . . . .

Long gone, vanished, obliterated and left for dead

so soon shall I be

As I suffocate there is no solace, no consolation

so I betray myself and whisper "I love you . . ."

and wait for my heart to finally rest

Falling Flying and Floating

I give you all of me
and I let it bounce around inside you
Whirlwind around
Believe me it's safe to see
These shackles are no longer on
and I'm after you

She says I love you
and it's the sweetest sound
my heart practically falls to the ground
It skips each time I see her
Before we confess our dire sins
and afterwards we celebrate our desperate desire

Hope it never stops for you
Want to see you in the red light
Your skin wet in the night
Digging your fingers into my naked back
Trickling down
This is ours
And you say I'm inside you
Drifting further each and every day

We can get silly in our own way
and this adoration is thick
and if you hide behind a secret wall
I'll break it down with my steel big boots
and take you away from all this madness
One day we won't have to live in this lie
but for today it's the only solution
I'll hold out for the revolution in your heart
May that be the resolution

On the brink
I stand on the edge with you
and I feel like throwing myself over with no regrets
and falling with you
I'll never stop falling
So give me you hand and let us glide down together
Feels like we're floating
and there's something special in the dark horizon
Let us piece together the mystery
or be surprised by the wonder of it all
Come down to the ground without a sound
Our feet gentle on the surface
Kiss me and let it all fade

CARRIED AWAY

And now I know what it's like to be blind
to be helpless and weak
to be useless and meek
I'm the docile creature that's
been blinded by your brightness
Witness fragility fragmented and broken
Shattered once again
I'm pretty sure these bends and breaks will never end
but it'll be ok as long as there's someone
to pick up these pieces and carry them away
or sweep me under your bed hoping to forget
this mess you've made

I'm the burden festering beneath your mattress
It's an unruly mess here
among other jagged memories and faces long forgotten
I hope to avoid this oblivion that
inevitably claims us all
Summoning all my might to avoid
becoming just another lost obscurity
meandering through this
pile of condemned words and feelings
Please, I beg, don't leave me here
I don't belong with such despicable company
I swear I don't!

I'm the shards of forgotten dreams and
beliefs that have been discarded by others
Rejected, defeated, unrequited
Though I wait patiently, hopelessly, to one day be carried away
and perhaps pieced back together

or stripped down to the very
core of my soul
Praying that you won't let me fall
Whatever the future may bring
Whether it be guile some and mean
Something glorious and pristine
or maybe something in between
I know I won't be prepared
for life is war
And it flanks us with hate and love
with betrayal and hope
with death and despair
It's left many scares across my bruised body
Some shallow, some deep
Some still needing time to heal
And unfortunately there's much more to life
And much more to feel
And sometimes it's too much to bear
And nobody seems to care

So after it beats me bloody
after it denies me my desires
and rips my heart
twisting the Knife in my back oh-so-slowly
till the pain ricochets through my
body leaving me tortured
and withering on the ground begging for death,
Will someone be there to pick me up . . . .
I hope one day
someone will have the strength
to carry me away

DRUG SONNET

My brain's a mass of incandescent shit
While I'm lifted up after a shy high
My veins constrict—Ow my dick, I'm lit
Ha! Ha! Laughing with affliction, I lie
Can't kick this shit—Damn, just one hit?
Oh man, this blue dream is grander than sky
I'm a carousel, while I throw a fit
I'm spun, my splitting synapses cry
I'm weeping I'm sleeping—Wait What, Where is it?
I'm not losing my mind, just one more try
It's swimming in the acid! Catch it!
Rescue me while I let out one last sigh
Oh No! my God I can't find my head
I let my mind wander and now I'm dead

DEATH IN A PUBLIC JOHN

Masturbating in the public restroom at 10:50 AM
What an addiction this has become
Disgustingly Disgusting
Yet pleasingly perverse
I couldn't even finish my breakfast
I'm chewing as I'm strokin' my very best
Yes, Yes, Yesssssss!!!

Shit, Fuck!
My inspiration was thrown off
Inhaling too quickly
My breath is leaving me
No, not like my freakin' wife did
I'm choking
I'm suffocating
Damn that damn damn crispy sweet bacon
Damn it to hell!!!
Probably where I'm headed after this
What went wrong, whose to blame?
Must be my malfunctioning glottis
My wind pipe is stuffed full of greasy bacon
With my Head in my Hand—
Gasping for air—
Oxygen please enter my nose!
Caress the vulva in my mouth!
Oh God, is this the final climax?
My last thrill?

Well, here we go!

Getting off on affixation

Slamming down on the poor wrinkled guy

I'm getting so dizzy from pleasure, or lack of air

Not really sure which

But before the blackness engulfs me forever

No meaningful life flashes before my eyes

Right before I die

Right before skeeting all over the bathroom stall wall

Right over where someone has written:

If this is the end, then truly what's there to hope for

Right before this deranged darkness comes to take me forever

I think one incredibly stupid thought

"Oh how I wish I listened to my Rabbi. That psychic told me fat would be the death of me. Goddamn you Bacon. Fuck you bacon . . . ."

And then as I fall my head slams across the shit-encrusted lid,

creating a sick mixture of reddish-brown splattering across the stall floor

Gross, I scared the shit out of myself without even noticing

My eyes flicker,

Once,

Twice,

3,000 times,

And die a painfully horrendous death in a public John

LOST BUT NOT GONE

Missing you is always the easiest thing to do
Even though you've been long gone
The spirit within you
Leaves nothing that can't be done
And when you were near me I could feel it
I couldn't deny it

This unquenchable feeling that drains most everyone else
This unbelievable sensation that comes only when you come
This unescapable destiny that leaves me doomed
This unspeakable truth

Don't dare ponder it
My perception is not like yours
My discernment is different
In different
No nihilist am I
No sadist
Apathetic misanthrope has got me pegged
or am I still lost
Meandering the wrong alleys in my own mind

Have I got them crossed this time

Mixed up

Ready for there demise

Subconscious suicide and then hilarity can ensue

Bemused?

Of course!

Just the ruminations of a madman on the brink

Knowing it's a celebration when we link

Under the water I sink

So I tear at my hair

Buyers beware

He grilled that sucka like a 6 ounce

and it made a sickening noise when his skin peeled

but it was all a dream

A deranged dream

Better though than this nightmare

So routine, redundant, ridiculous

Yes, you could say it's all been done

At least three times

But nothing compares to the real thing

so stick the needle in

Jumping Into the Sun

This is exactly as it should be
As the sun burns in my eye's reflection
So bright so beautiful
The reason for our existence
And this mission to the stars and beyond
To save all that's worth saving
I know that you're praying
I can see you kneeling by your bed before you go to sleep
Keep me safe, you ask of God, in your subtle words
But there's nothing he can do
This is my sacrifice
May it suffice
So that it may be the end
or to put it better: a new beginning
Another chance
To get it right
Put up a decent fight
A future so bright
—Oh, what a sight!

I am the denouement
The ending to this tragic story
but when you remember me
don't let tears fall to the floor
Just look to the wondrous sky
Thank God, you're alive
We found a way to survive
Barely keeping this world alive

The surface is bubbling and the activity is incredible

Hotter than fire

I contemplate melting

or the alternative

Neither is really enticing

Thoughts race through my head

My life flashes before my irises

Everything, from my father's pugnacious drawl to my wife's pea green eyes, and my

daughter's fragile hands . . . .

I hope they can forgive me for leaving them

They didn't understand

This enormous feat

Mine to accomplish

It's my destiny, you must see

To die so that others may live

It's the only way

I can't go back now

Past the point of no return

Hold on, Hold on with all my might

Incandescent light

Gleaming, shimmering, shining

I'm not lying

This is exactly as it should be

Going out with a bang louder than life itself

NOTHING WOULD BE ENOUGH

I'm drowning in the darkness

and no one is there to hear my suffocation

I've been abandoned

Forgotten

Seen through

Memories entwined and lost

Saccharine and melancholy

and everything oh so holy

but if I see a gleam

will it be to late

What is my fate?

And is it running out?

Faster I know, like time bomb tick tick ticking

Knowing all I'll have left are these . . . .

And is it enough-

May it be what is needed to survive

Could it be?

Pull the trigger

Let's see

Will I be absolved?

Do I have the gumption

What it takes

Shall I embrace this abyss

Or is it the counterpart

And all my hope leads to this pinnacle

Open your eyes and live and remember to feel alive

Carry on and you will believe

It will be sufficient

but nothing may be enough

Nothing would be enough

I'm Waiting

I have no empathy for you
because I've never been there
but I'm very sorry for you
Don't you see what we've done
what we've become
and will this oblivion eat up my insides
with pride I'm waiting
May the curtain between us and heaven be lifted
I hear your heart beat in the distance
but it fills my ear drums like canons exploding
During an atrocious war that killed thousands
and will we count ourselves among the casualties
Among the fallen
Did you hear me calling for you
Did they sound like faint whispers
Did they ever reach the supernal skyline
or the subtle horizon upon I know I saw you walking
Are you searching for me like I searched for you
with honor I'm waiting
Will I just turn to dust below your feet
-No, I will be there scavenging the wastelands for you
Distraught forlorn and weary
An arrow crossed in my heart

I want to take you far away to a brand new place

Identities erased

I'll look into you face

and know just who you are

and you'll smile

It brings all the light we need

and everything's just right

We'll never have to fight

And the curtain thickens

My legs turn to lead

All I feel is dread

You're lost but not gone

At least I hope your hearts still flapping like a bird that's trapped inside a wire cage

I want to let you free

waiting for you to fly right back to me

and we can be free

I'll no longer starve for your kisses

A profound urge that goes down to the core

Press your lips against mine, burning

and we can forget all that keeps us down

Learning to mourn the dead in the ground

Instead of counting our loses

Know that they're safe and sound

And our faith in them is as strong as lightning bolts in the eye of a storm

In disbelief I'm waiting

Horrible and Abhorrent

This oppression must cease
This diabolical arm against my chest
Covering my heart
Masking all which is beautiful
This is worse than it seems
Opening secret drawers
and finding hiding places
Just look at your faces
No more . . . .
It can't go on like this
". . . Horrible . . ." she said
and me just sitting passive, stoic, and stupid
seething white-
but no more . . . .
You shouldn't cage a bird
and you can't cage me
Fighting for freedom every single day
Wishing there was some other way
If you'd only open your eyes just a little
and see that I'm really okay
or is this dissolution imminent
Are these walls completely crumbled
Does everything have to change
Be re-aranged and deranged

I'm leaving now
as I should be
'cause I just can't take
this no more

I am the forsaken son
The prodigal son
but I'm not the only one

So take my hand
and waste a little time with me
we can paint the world different colors
brown, and black, yellow, and blue
because I love you
even if you don't love me
This goodbye was never good enough
But it's all I will have
Snapped fingers and a glimmer in your eyes
A novel I could write for them and their deliberate waverings
but that wouldn't matter
Just something else . . . . *horrible* and abhorrent

RED LOCKS CARESS THE WORLD

The scent of flowers is intoxicating
Or something else in the air
Our bodies can float
Ride the sky
And absorb the rays from the sun
Squinting we can see forever
See what we want
Be what we want
Time is eternal
So spend some time with me
Come under my canopy
Where we can be free
No atrocity

Meander down this path
Pristine in shadows and cascading light
Let the trees decide what comes through
Everything will be alright
As long as I have you
Embrace the night
When it comes
The stars blink for us
Let your feet mix in the dirt
Let go of anything that hurts
Because it's not worth holding

Get your nails dirty
Be rambunctious
Be unruly
Scratch the bark and leave your sign
Everything will be just fine
Cross your arms
Scrunch your nose
Be bewildered
Be baffled
Leave a mark in the sand
Take my hand
And let the tide wash it away
Knowing you'll never fade away

Remember the memories, twisted
Somehow we'll all be lifted
I'll pick a rose and lay it down
Upon all the places we have found
Fond freckles will litter the ground
Red locks caress the world

THE BLUE IN YOU/AS I FALL

I ask if you could possibly give me less
you demure and say yes
and these fallacies go on forever
as these angels turn into demons
and they circle my bed
and creep into my head
The things they said
cannot be forgotten

My anger swells
as I dwell
on all the mistakes
like empty crates
without purpose
with you face pressed up against the glass
I pull your hair
you wouldn't dare?
and the regrets are like numerous cuts upon my wrist
stinging

But I've got you in my sights
the cross hairs cut your eyes
like the lies that tore at my heart strings
like the sealed septum just broke open
Bursting at the seams
each suture separating silently
But you could fix it
like the needle couldn't
shouldn't
so sleep an unintoxicated dream
where we can be together
where the smoke floats forever
and the clouds look like whatever we want them to
and the blue in you is deep
so let it seep into me
so that you are alright
at least for tonight
Give it all to me
Let my veins consume it all
I'd take this fall
Come crashing down harder than ever
Through floor boards and mud
Through pavement and earth
Just to show you
what your worth

So We'll See

Broken like the capillaries in your eyes
like the many deaths that we all die
while the violins play a sad song
it goes on and on like the lazy path of a blindman
A fear that goes back decades
and isn't it the same old story
Riding the train into the light
Devastating disaster
and nothing I did could stop it that night

Like the blood trickling down your prettiest knife
after it stabbed those hearts
Fast and without meaning
Just flowing
Obeying the laws
Innocence turned vicious and malicious
Callous and mean
Apathetic
Sick-
Dick-

Need a break from all this

Needing to take it all in for a little while

Remembering to smile

even while I'm getting the hell out of here

My dear

I know you'll forgive me

Remembering that pressed purple flower in your room

and all that time we spent in my room

and how you left me there

Tears on the ground

Making no sound

Except for a heart breaking

leaking

and somehow it keeps seeking

Like a wounded warrior that won't rest until the reaper himself appears

and even then the angel of death might waver or just take me to her

then I can carry her back home

and call it the end beneath the willow tree

or so we'll see

LET ME

Her skin is wet like a river flowing

as she digs her nails into my back

Growing

and the skin is shredded

and her eyes are like twinkling stars

Burning into me

She is melting me

She ignited

and now I'm melting

Watch as I dissolve

right before your eyes

your beautiful eyes

Blue like the sky before a storm

that's knocked down every goddamn tree in it's path

Calm like the tranquility that comes after the end is done

And a new beginning is forged

Fading into you for the first time

and you kissed my neck shyly

"Nice to meet you" I think on the verge of something grander

Let me take her hand down this weary path and learn somehow to forget the past

Let me-

Let this love be the only drug we need

I feel it course through my veins like you would not believe

Have I found my Eve

Let me-

Dance around the raging fire while you can

and when the embers finally vanish

after the time that's be cherished

I hope you'll remember me

because I know I won't forget you too soon

Solemnly knowing my chances are slim

but certainly, for once, I deserve to win

By the Skin of Our Teeth

My smile is crooked but it doesn't mean I'm a crook

My eyes are dark but it doesn't mean I can't look into the light

My stories long like a meandering book

I have to fight to keep my sight

and the irony is I never had it

So the blackness consumes me

but hidden within is something

There is something I can see

and then the revelations peel my eyelids open

I see what I want to see

Creating something where once there was nothing

and it's a somber ritual

That breathes life into everything

and maybe if it can save you

It won't have all been in vain

Such a shame

This silly game

Breaks me down time and time again

Again

That sliver of moon just for us

Waning

Where the light gets in

Reminiscing on the Red sunset that continues to burn in my mind

Give me a sign

And make it simple and legible

Because this quest has me fatigued

Flailing failure

Somewhat lost with trembling hands

So take me and we'll avoid this catastrophe

By the skin of our teeth

RETURN TO ME

As I walk down this solitary path
I'm more somber than I should be
So I scrape at the walls
I try to take them down
I'm walking through walls trying to get to you
I squint my eyes hoping you're not gone
My fists bang against the stone
I don't want to miss you anymore
but what else is there to do
when I love you
and my tears start to overwhelm the ducts
I try to keep them back
but I can't
there's nothing I can do
They start to fall down my cheeks as I'm tearing at the walls
Like acid my tears burn through the floor and I'm falling
For you I start calling
To come rescue me
Be my savior
Will you ever hear me?
Please pull me down
Or am I just falling to the ground
My life starts to flash before my eyes
Waiting for my eye sight to fade
but instead I splash down

The water is clear but I'm discouraged

There's a lack of color here

because you're not here

In indignation I scream your name

I plea for you to come home

It's easy to find

I'm following you there

because we felt something and it could last forever

So come and dance with me in heaven

It's in your eyes

and in the ten thousand lies

in our minds we don't have to say

Let our love devour it all

and it'll be beautiful

A splendor like we've never seen before

So tie anchors to my feet

and let the surface of the water rise above my nose

This sweet suffocation will suit me fine without you

I'm rushing down

and the bubbles are streaming from my mouth

I close my eyes wanting to give up forever

but then I see your apparition appear before me

may it be real or a hallucination from the lack of oxygen doesn't matter

It still gives me strength to keep on searching for you

may I come out the other side underneath a beautiful sun

or a moon casting shadows until you finally return to me

BEAUTIFUL CRIME

Palpitate, Palpitate
Cut my wrist
Bleed to Death
Life Disaster
fly Away
To a place of minimal Decay
Nothing to fear
ugly eyes
Lies Lies and more Lies
Purple nails scratch my neck
Tear and shred silky skin
Reviving one wish
To be stabbed Again
Again, Again through the heart
Loving beauty is a crime
Palpitate, Palpitate
Slit my eyes
Thankfully Blind
Loving beauty is a crime

Tasting Oblivion

I breath this smoke into you
A dire excuse to kiss you
Don't stay away from me
You see
like I see
In your eyes we can be
Not trapped or hurt
Borrowed and bleeding
As you caress my face
my hands dance
Flowing into each other
Like an epic dance
Moving in unison
Take my hand and move it where it belongs
Where it longs to be
For so much time now
It echoes in the past and I feel the trepidation
but not this time
because her butterflies can fly with mine
and it'll be something so divine
when the inspiration hits
a muse with blond locks
—take it and run
because it has begun
and it's like the most glorious song that can ever be sung
so breathe this smoke and let it fill your lungs
and what may come will come

Like the blue in you consuming me
Let it engulf us
and we'll lay for eternity

Could I crush on you?
without smothering you
like a pillow pressed against your face
and I'm holding it so tight
my knuckles are white
like the whites of your blue eyes
paper thin walls where you can hear every sound
In your brain I'm tearing down all the boundaries
and I'm reaching up towards the sky
holding you under the stars
Keeping you warm like the sun
that brings us all the incandescence
and even though I'm lying
I tell you I love you
and kiss your soft lips, dying
Giving in to something unknown
An oblivion worth tasting

GUILTY

Does it hurt like it should
Could it
Like cutting a wrist
Like sticking a needle in
Wicked sin
Maybe I should cry for help
and would you hear me
Does anyone care?
The profound yearning
This is what I'm learning
and I'm yours in your arms
Your face pressed against me
Breathless you kiss me
Fill this void and make it beautiful
Make it like you
Under the stars
Or is it your eyes
Dream it clearly
and keep it like a secret
something precious, beloved
Loved, fits like a glove
Auburn
Let it burn
and breathe it in
without consequence
and then let's get in the water
It's warm but it giving me shivers
Under the surface give me your hand

Damn

Man

Lovesick and drowning

Can you feel the surge

or is it just my imagination

Running away with me

Prepared to wait for you

Underneath this vine

We can swing

This time is something so divine

Let it shine

Like the reflection off the water

In it I see us

Like the future etched in the waves

Each one striking serenely against our moist skin

Yours like silk draped around me

Want to wear you like a cape and be your hero

Or a blanket to keep me forever warm

Hand in hand we dive down

Forgetting for a moment the world above us

No lingering hurt or horrible desire

So hold me beneath like a handgun

and pull the trigger if you want

Just have no regrets

and Get Set

Don't forget

I remember how you told me you loved me

and I was afraid to do the same

But the sweetest lie I ever told left my lips

Was it enough for you?

Crazy how, it wound up being true

I'm guilty and it kills me

GLOVES

Taciturn and in control

Nothing escapes me

Ready for the unexpected

For the blood stained on my face

In the mirror I see the reflection, the deep red and piercing eyes

Time for the gloves

for Love

Let them keep my hands clean

The things that I have seen

Redemption rings resolutely

I puncture the air

and remember the oblivion of her pink lips

How she bit mine

but don't cross the line

Time for the gloves

for Love

I take you and I squash you

Like a bug till you explode your green upon the walls

or I'll take this gun and press it against your lips

Let's pull the trigger

This is our fate

Your heart must stop its beating

Be destroyed

Let your face cave in

Bite the curb and I'll stomp you out

or light a flame under you and watch you burn away

like I burn for her

She is haunting me

Her silhouette cast a shadow upon my bedroom wall

I walk through this never ending hall

and become one with her darkness

An Angel Through Closed Eyes

I close my eyes, and try to forget

Forget the lies being told

The harm being distributed

Easier said than done

Yet easy enough to do

I open my eyes expecting a foreign world to appear

Sharp lights stab at my irises

I look around, everything seeming abstruse

I am in a room

Alone

A white room, no windows, no doors

I begin to shiver, I must be scared

I collapse on the floor

This can't be happening, I'm too young

I jump towards the wall and start clawing at it in a ferocious fit

My fingernails begin to chip off against the wall

I stop and lay my hands by my side, Fingers dripping

I must seek salvation!

Follow the same path that brought me here

I close my eyes again

This time I see a face

The word beautiful would not do the face justice

Would be the harshest crime

No such word could describe the sight

Certainly a supernal vision

An Angel for me to see

An Angel to wear my heart around her neck

An Angel it must be

Hopefully no disguise is being worn

But I'm still in the room

Deathly White

Yet I feel the presence of an Angel

What does this mean?

Is treachery in my future?

Who cares!

I'll just close my eyes

I'll just lay here blinded

Comforted by a beautiful panoply

A heavenly dream

An Angel Through Closed Eyes

An Explosion In the Sky

Here I lay
Where the silence is beckoning
I can't feel a thing
As it courses through my limbs
and you run in the other direction
further and further away from me
a thousand miles or more
you fucking whore
no, I can't feel a thing
and it keeps on coming
yes, I start coming
and no one can stop it

I'm a pariah
people's pupils pierce mine
and they see nothing divine
see right through my x-ray skin
what a sin

And yet again this silence captivates
Thrills, chills
Floats on like the most elusive dream
Changing everything it touches
And it may be the answer

My mouth runs off
stumbles and falls
down every single hallow
Dreading the west coast
Scared of that ghost
Out of my mind
It can be so kind

Then that calliopean slam
and Damn
it's over
The angels are dead
disgraced over what has been said
and the celebration in the streets for death
Preaching darkness
Achieving the perfect kill
And what may come will amaze us all
with jaws gaping wide
An explosion in the sky
On a perfect day
Let out one last sigh
and hold love tight
Look at the light
with trembling hands
It'll be alright in the incandescent light

AWE AND REDEMPTION

Should I lay here and succumb to my somnolence
My dreams: a landscape of awe and redemption
or give in to this concupiscent state of mind
This nubile girl thinks the latter
shall I make her mine
Walking this solitary path I mutter
"Please believe in me . . ."
and so we'll see
I've been buried before
The ash lingers in my eyes
and the flames have burnt out
Burn out
Lacking the motivation for anything
Except the pills pills pills
You shit-faced fucks should get away from me
Because I don't see the things the way you see
but we can agree
These lies cut deep
and your eyes are getting clear now
while mine remain

How have they been?

What have they seen?

Something obscene?

A candle lit scene

and hazel eyes dancing

flowers at our feet

the music playing in the background

but it's almost like there's no sound

Pausing for a moment in time

It was so kind

But there's so much more

and at times it's almost too much to bear

and those are the times I cherish the most

Running my hands through her hair

How much I cared

And the carnival lights are flickering, fading, faulting

So kiss me in the darkness

Let us prolong this madness

Like the talking fish promised

Look into the eyes of God

and perhaps you'll see your reflection

THIS LAND, MY LAND

Through this deserted wasteland of pain and misery I travel
I shamble through these dark alleys
forgotten voices, and stirring echoes greet me
dire eyes, and crystal smiles betray me
I step through broken hearts
and I dig through unrequited love
I search for the one thing that will keep me going
that will help me survive
that will keep me from perishing
the pain around me trembles
making the world around me shatter
leaping, and twisting I long to escape from this land of pain
in the distance in the horizon I see a faint glimpse of hope
the world around me starts to crumble
wounded souls fall around me trying to bring me down with them
I twist away from them
I close my eyes, and shudder as the world dies around me
pleads of anguish greet me from all sides
I freeze, and my mind begins to flutter
I close my eyes tighter, squeezing the tears from my eyes
I see a hideous face in my mind, distorted and disfigured
I close my eyes tighter, my temples throbbing, blood falls from my irises
blood flows down my cheeks, and my wounded soul begins to heal
my crying heart, begins to heal as well, as it bleeds all the pain away
the blood and tears hit the ground and stain the floor beneath me

I wallow in my own pain, surrounded, trapped by it once again

I lift myself up off of the pain soaked floor, breaking the essence of pain

my eyes, bloodshot and blurry, see something in the distance

in the distance I see two beckoning eyes, calling to me

I run, in hopes of escaping this dreaded land

two beautiful eyes stare directly at me, I am engulfed by there beauty

suddenly fear sets in, and I ruminate about the eyes in front of me

good or evil, I ask myself

will these eyes bring me pain

will they destroy hope

or will they be the thing I was looking for

the thing I need to survive

will these eyes keep me alive

will they help me to escape this world of pain

I hope they do, or I may be forever doomed and enslaved to this world

this land of pain and misery

this land where I have lived for years

this land I long to escape

this land, my land

THE END OF ME

Shattered
Screaming because I can't take this pain no more
Again this vicious cycle unleashes its reigns of mayhem upon me
where chaos rules supreme
and the hurt goes on everlastingly
like an angel dying
this is nothing to dismiss
her kiss
Sailed
Gone for good
and another scar to burn on my skin
Her heart is hard as stone
I could feel it deep in my bones
So rough that it cut me deep
And my blood leaks for her
Longs to sweep her up into this kind oblivion
Can I even be your memory?
And is that all I have left of you
It plays like a slide show in my mind
Moments frozen in time
And I couldn't make you mine
How you shine
like a diamond
In this ugly world you were beautiful
For a fleeting second we were perfect souls
hand in hand
and now again I have this hole
I've taken this fall
with no one to catch me
and the pavement is beckoning
Sickening
Consumed by this madness
This undisclosed urge

Did I ever mean anything
Something
While you meant everything
and you just walked away
as my heart broke
Are the cracks beginning to show
Each one dividing something so irreplaceable
Slicing my soul
Each tear echoes so loud in my mind
Trying to put the past behind
Walk away like you did
Each step took you further and further away from me
and I have nothing left of you
How I wish I had something
A picture to keep hidden
but all I have is within
and it's dissipating
because I cannot hold on any longer
I broke the shiny diamond and I deserve this
All my careful plans and ploys devastated
Eradicated and Destroyed
Lord knows I can't take anymore
Demons and psychic pain with no one to blame
Insane
Such disdain
Such anger turned within
Inexplicable Sin
Things I wish I could forget
Board up like an abandoned house
Burn it to the ground
Regret all the things you've found
Cut the lines on the sidewalk
and mourn this loss in the dark
Because this end has no new beginning
It is simply the end of me

NOTHING BETTER

I like how you climb me
like a mountain
and I know you can reach higher
and together we can achieve anything
This terrain is new
and I'm no longer lost
even if I'm standing in the rain
waiting for you

And we dance
and your curves are dangerous
I drive on them and surely I'll crash
and burn
Never forgetting to burn
oh, and how it feels this time
To yearn
So I'm cherishing each second with or without you

Bursting from beneath
Out of the dark
My nails dirty
Leaving it all behind in the mud
and I'm finally on top of it all
and one tear drop falls
I look to the brilliant sky
let out a long sigh
thank God I'm alive
and pray

Black flowers blossom in my heart

Gentle impulsion

Feels like a resurrection

and all this time I've been dead

I finally said I love you again

and I can only imagine what the future holds

a taste of creation

passionate discords and whispers

Even the ethereal dreams of intoxication

Bring yourself to the surface

Let me see your face

and how you look at me

leaves me paralyzed and longing

Hard enough to look away as is

but how do you look away when an angel looks right at you

Trapped in her gaze

Not just a silly phase

Attached and you can say what you want

You will hurt my feelings

But it's alright you're forgiven

And it's this crazy heart that is being driven

Crashing into walls and going down wrong way streets

but you're the road I'm on and I'm swerving

Just drunk enough to drive you home

or where ever we want to go

A piano is weeping

Forget about it all for a little while, seeping

she don't mind she don't care

and it's something special to share

I wouldn't be a liar anymore if I told you that-

The sea is above us this time, believe me

and there is truly nothing better

Than hiding in your shadow

KILL OUR VILLAINS

Your eyes whisper to me
something wonderful and serene
how they speak to me
and what they say can't be spoken
but you can try
and we can die
and I'll blame it on my own sick pride

Maybe we are a different breed
This is something you must take heed
We are unique, indeed
and together we are an unstoppable force
Adam with his Eve
and there's no one to deceive
and although the snake is menacing
He can't touch our love
It's something sacred
His lies and disingenuous ways
It can go on for days
but still we are stronger
hand in hand
we can stand
against it all
No devastating fall

Just one more chance we've been granted

A chance to get it right

and I see you in the incandescent light

You're beautiful

I won't get it wrong this time

I can't get it wrong this time

Finding a way to call you mine

oh, and how you shine

Like a star in the distance

So I reach for the closest one

It's become an addiction

To feel the burn

An affliction that runs deep

A lesson never learned

Here where everything is white

We can be untouchable

A marvelous sight

and we don't have to be alone anymore

One day we'll rise up

and it'll be easier on you

We'll be clean like glycerin

with no lingering need

no craving to feed

And even though you'll surely pierce my heart

Waiting in the dark for it to silently explode

May the bullet pass through and kill all our villains

Giants in the Sky

You've seared my flesh with your burning kisses
It's them that I'm missing
Are you listening?
Like falling for the first time
Just know that it'll only hurt like it should
This love is perspicuous
and your lips are something delicious
I taste you
You're a ruby and I like red

I watch you sleep
A soundless sound that is so beautiful
and it's like the world's muted when you're not around
Your emotions have an echo
and I'm consumed by it
Like a wave let it wash over me
Let me float on the salt
Walking on water
thinking I'm in control
but knowing it's just an illusion
A magnificent fallacy
I chose to believe in

As the lights go down
I hold you closer
and I've never felt so alive
This feeling you've given me
cannot be expressed with a thousand words
Though I'll try and try and try

Soaked in you
I drink you in
Between these two glimmering walls
Laying with you
Content to die with you
and these chemicals are so amusing
Climb you like a beanstalk
Reaching for the giants in the sky
Cover you like a blanket
Cozy beneath the blue sun
Let your vision pierce the fog and we can have a home in the clouds

WELCOME YOUR GHOST

Without you I'm like a junkie
Itching and convulsing
and I can't wait for my next fix
How sickening
Love me like the drug
Need me
Crave me
Be lost without me

Be my deep blue Ferris-wheel
and let me ride you for hours
for a penurious fee
and we can be free
My blood pumping fierce
Can you feel my heart beat?
Stuck in deadly rhythm
Panic for me because I have everything to lose
Hysteria in her voice
What I burn is my choice
I am the sun shinning bright

Can you see the light?

and you would be a glorious sight

in my black and blue arms

I grab and reach for you

but only end up buried

Have you disappeared

How are you invisible?

and is our love divisible

Is it dissipating faster than air sucking into our lungs

or is it everlasting

Still here after you're gone

And your laughter leaves behind an echo in my heart

Wish I could stay here with you in the dark

but the light is coming to take you away

The day that's almost as gorgeous as you

With your golden locks wrapped around me

Wrap yourself tighter

Don't be afraid of my suffocation

It's impossible for your love to crush me

But will you just end up buried

Underneath the brown soil

I've taken for granted the shortness of our lives

So fragile fleeting flagrant

I welcome your ghost with open arms

Haunt me forevermore

OBLIVION IS GONE

This darkness overwhelms me

and this oblivion is long gone

taken for granted or corrupted

The embers that burnt so bright are dying out

and I have nothing left to hold on to

I feel like giving up

giving in

giving out

surrendering to my ominous fate

raising the white flag for all to see

will anyone be there to take it

shake it, break it

do what you will

because these regrets sting like a wild fire out of control

and it burns so bright sometimes

Reminds me of you

and this abandonment leaves my soul in shreds

there is nothing left

and I wish I could say that that was all okay

and that everything is going to be alright

But the fogs rolling in
As black as the night
Let it envelop me
Wrap me up like you once did
and I'll do my hardest to pretend
this cadence isn't killing me
Like putting a gun to my head
and pulling the trigger tightly and firmly
Painting the walls with my brains
Letting the blood drip casually
and will there be anyone there to mournfully cover me up
When I'm so far gone
because I've been so far down
I won't make a sound
or welcome this demise
and maybe one day I'll rise
Become a cloud drifting in the sky
letting in slivers of sunshine
Warming the small of your back

LIGHTNING

Teetering on the edge of nothingness
This numinous atmosphere
where I don't need air to breath
where we can be whatever we imagine
I ask if you want to come with me
You nod your head diligently
Can we reach the stars without burning
Something we'll have to try
Learning to die
Only your words can kill me anyhow
or the absence of any
God knows there's been plenty
but they'll never become abundant or enough
In due time maybe we'll see what it is we really need
Though there's barely any time left really
To say all that needs to be said
I may be better off dead
But will my words shatter the silence
Like a chandelier falling to the ground
Even I know it's going to bring us down
and I won't be able to rise by myself
and I may be all alone by then

So I'll say my solemn goodbye and be off
Remember the good times we had
All the way back to that youthful boy I was
That stupid town we call home
How all along I was just a bit player in a movie starring you
but it's okay
because it's hypnotizing
So I'll just lose with eloquence and remember how you sung that song
and it left me paralyzed
Will my officious goodbye suffice or matter in the end
I peer down over the edge
It's beautiful
I was always just stumbling around when I was with you
Watching those suns go down
Inhaling smoke with our heads down
Elated sedated satiated
Watching the world go by
Something electric
and our time is running out
I'd be lying if I didn't say it's something so frightening
For you are like lightening
and you struck me so hard

NEVER BE ALONE

Look into my future and my past
and I hope you'll see yourself there
even when things get hard
know that I'm here to stay
far and away
You're a star shinning bright
Your lights light me on fire
and I love the way it burns
Deepest desire
Nothing can extinguish it
How it shines
I say "I love you babe
and do you feel the same
I don't want to play no games"
It could be a shame
This answer on the tip of you tongue
but it could be something magical
Divine
Something precious, practically mythical
Something digital, not habitual
Blood feels my mouth
From keeping it shut

Waiting, Waiting, Waiting

For them to all float on those clouds you sliced with your vision

and is there space for us below it all

Hope they don't crush us one day

or will we just fall off the earth

Careening over the edge, I know it'll be beautiful in the end

Like a beautiful curtain letting in a sliver of sunshine reflecting in your eyes and there's

no lies beneath the violent blue

I hear your laughter and I forget it all anyway

I'd give it all to you any day and I do

I remember when I first kissed you

Sparks flew from our lips like rockets

and the embers are still burning

For you I'm yearning

We can go on

Just you and I in the sky

Just let out one last sigh

Even if you're not quite ready

Let the air fill your lungs

and sink into my skin

and we'll never be alone again

NEVER LET YOU GO (SEARCHING)

I wander these landscapes aimlessly, hopelessly
Searching
Sometimes I'm a ghost and everyone sees right through me
but truly I'm the one that's haunted
Sometimes I'm a parasite clinging for life on to another
but truly I'm the one that's getting the life sucked from me
and I'm disappearing
so I solemnly sign my name in the dirt
and hope someone will come upon it and know
that once I existed
I was more than a skeleton
More than skin and bones
A part of some grand machine-
      rusted, corroded, barely functioning
      some elaborate plan
      etched across the sky
With purpose and determination I continue
Searching
and though I'm fatigued I won't stop
because there's something inside that won't let me
Could it be a perfect memory
Our lips pressed against each others, struggling to get it right
Lying together for hours in the night, abandoning our fears
I'll save your tears

Create a river we can float down like veins stretching out in a body

and we don't have to be heartbroken anymore

Our scars just paint pretty pictures of the past

and nostalgia here is a beautiful thing

That doesn't bring us down but lifts us up

Towards the effervescent sun

And from there I can see it all

I'm truly in heaven

I'm like a cloud floating

Cutting across the sky

but I know that eventually I'll just plummet towards the earth

and will someone catch me before I crash and smash into a million pieces

Pick me up and keep me safe

and I'll forgive you for the delay

I barely made it to this day

It feels like I've been buried for so long, endless decay

Better off gone

and it's all such a waste

but when I get you in my sights I'll never let you go again

STRONGER

This crazy head has led me here
and I feel I can't forget the past
it's such a waste
all of it
It feels so natural to just give it up
Would I be missed?
What of those I kissed?
What would happen if I turned the last page
Yes, I'm the rat stuck in the cage
and I can't shake these feelings
Reckless and lost
Need something to hold on to
but nothing's there
Does anyone care?

These bleeding wrists have made their choice
fess up you messed up kid
you got nothing left anyways
and the future is bleak
it's no one I seek
dreams out of reach
condemned and left for dead

Sweating bullets in the rain

what can soothe this pain?

Let gravity pull the tears down

In a world that's lacking sound

I'll kneel on the ground

Beg for an answer

Beg for solution, some retribution

I scream like a madman and look to the lifeless sky

Don't you know there's a storm rolling in

and none of us will be prepared

I'd take you there

Underneath the soil and worms

Locked in a box that I fixed with radiating light

Let it be all the light we need

We can plant a seed

and watch what grows?

the sky is velvet black

and I ask you if you can see it too

you nod and tell me you love me

as I take you in for one last embrace

may the sun collide into the moon

and break down through our atmosphere

Together we can catch it

Hold it up and keep it safe

Let it be what we need it to be

Don't you see?

Now you can see

With eyes of marble roll it around

let your teeth carve the grass

and let it be a message for all to witness

We are stronger than this

TINY CITIES MADE OF ASHES

I got to remember
to remember how you forgot me
Didn't keep me in your heart
though your lies painted pretty pictures in the dark
How you tore down the photos on the wall
I watched you always stupefied
I watched you laugh and cry
Pump yourself full of drugs
Dose after dose
What have you lost?
and all the while I was there
Looking into you dilated eyes
Wide blue eyes like quicksand
I drowned in them
and I can't breathe anymore
I was always breathless around you
gasping for air
waiting for the perfect moment to steal some
because you were the nicest thing I've ever seen
A broken angel struggling to survive
and now I'm inches from life
Trapped and stuck in limbo

Why did you put me here?

Waiting for the next one to bite the dust

Or tear down my walls with their feet

Nestle in the nooks and crannies in my skin

Live a lovely life with me

and we can play like children eternally

till my heart stops beating

or the world starts burning

Searing our flesh

Coming down around us while we stand defiantly

and I'll think to myself

I still love her

and when we rise together I hope I'll be able to find her

because I won't be kissing her goodbye

no matter how hard she tries

We can hold our hands tight and peer below at the tiny cities made of ashes

TOO FAR GONE

I broke down
with a swift punch to the wall
I lost my patience
for it all
Seems I don't need anyone
underneath the sun
but still my heart it breaks
a celebration of the worse kind
Can I lean on you?
Can you see my scar and make it disappear
it never belonged there in the first place
Can you make my life real
I'm just learning to feel
Replace my heart and my brain
because today my mind's not the same
Don't you realize how my brain has shifted
Do you want to come inside
See the chaos that ricochets through every inch
be careful not to flinch
I grin to keep it all together on the inside
everyday it get's harder
is this the way it's suppose to go
Scared of living
and staring into a sea of eyes

Can any of them help me
and do any need my help?
Let me stand near some
Let me tear down the fortresses between us
because inside I know we can be beautiful
or am I just naive
Should I stop believing
Tear these nails across the walls
and get the blood off the floor
Return to the halls
call it quits
because it's lonely and I have no where left to hide
but then I Died
I was reborn
With the strength to carry on
Because I know I'm not too far gone

TAKE COVER (CAPE)

I'm no one
I'm nothing special
just drag me around
Take me with you
wear me like a cape
be my hero
run, and let me blow behind you
or will I delicately fall to the floor
and will you pick me up
or let others pace on me
either way
will those you save remember the fleeting moment
when I was there
Around your neck clinging to you for life
Remember the strife
in the past
take it fast
and crush it to smithereens
Tell me what you've seen

Cut my fingers and let the blood leak

let it swirl down to the ground

mix with the cloth

don't be silly don't make a sound

Did you demolish everything

right wear I lay

on top of my weary face

or will you tie the lace

around my hand

Stop the blood from flowing

and keep an open mind

and somehow you will find

this world can be ours for a little while

Hold it in the palm of your hand while you stand proud

Be gentle and

don't let it fall

let the circles in your eyes catch the lies

squint, take cover and let your soul sing

LOBOTOMY

Lobotomize me and then rip the sutures out of my head
Lay me in bed
Left for dead
Is this how you want to help me
Lock me in a room for you amusement
Peer at me through the glass
and I'll ask
"How long will this last?"
Longer than any madman can imagine
and my eyes aren't vacant like theirs
They are dark but full of hope and promise
So make me a single promise
Catch me when I fall
and when you break it
-Take it, Shake it, Fake it-
For we are not normal
For we are fucked in the head
and we doze in our minds
and in our brains you'll find

The answer—cozy and nonchalant
but who knows the question
I long for a swift resurrection
from beneath the soil I'll rise
and you'll just lay me back down
Silently sliding downward
and I'll sleep forevermore
till I wake to a new world
where no one recognizes me
where I'm a stranger
and there is no danger
or am I just dreaming of a better place
with your reckless face
Make haste
before time runs out
and the oceans overflow
drowning all us miserable bastards
while the sky lights up beautifully
Bang!
May we learn to exist again

BURNING FOR SURVIVAL

The world is on my back
and it's cutting these shoulder blades
with it's jagged edges
It's not just black and white
There are shades
Blue, purple, pink, green and grey
I roll it down my arm
as blood drips slowly to the floor
Don't let me slip and fall
Who will you call
When the sky lights up
and the birds fly downward
Being pushed by gravity
Obeying the rules and regulations
Can I break the law
Find an epic solution
Hold this world in my palm
Squeeze it tight and keep it safe
Keep it calm
and never let it drop
And when it rotates fiercely out of control burning the lines
let it be a sign
Together we can survive

HOPE AND SMOKE FLOATS

As you breathe smoke into me
I hope for it to last forever
It swirls around us in a fleeting daze
As the clock ticks ticks furiously
The Pendulum swings swiftly
But the embers burn still—

You come calling, unpoetic soft utterances
Beautiful in it's own way
So let's not waste a precious second
Because our love echoes quietly
Like the twilight of those embers we fondly remember
Like recollections of past glory and triumphs

Take my hand as we glimpse into the future
And hope that it may be as glorious as your grandest dreams
With hope it can be accomplished
A hope resilient to fear and broken stories
Like nothing you've ever seen before
That's what the future can hold
Void of darkness and treachery and horrors untold
It can be brighter than any ones ever known—
Yes, it can be better than you know
If you'd let yourself believe it
So with trust in hand thrust yourself into the unknown
Knowing it will be alright
At least for tonight
And maybe the rest of your life

ADAM AND EVE

Did you hear the life drain from you

and was it the only solution

Let's try to start a bloodless revolution

Run through the streets hand in hand

and we'll try not to crash into the buildings or brick walls

Paint these towns whatever colors we please

and when the buildings tumble down I'll hold you up above it all

above the rumble and dust

I won't ever let you fall

May we start a paradise exempt of tyranny

Let us see with infinite clarity

Our love can be stronger than the hate that can consume

Let the rage float away

Push it out of yourself

For today is the best day of our lives

No more addictions to afflictions

Let me just stare into your extraordinary eyes

No more lies!

Just let out a long sigh

Let it waver through the night

and we'll look to the sky

Stare into the sun and try not to go blind

and as you pupils implode

One day we'll find this absurdity doesn't have to be true

We won't die alone

Not me and you

We'll stand on the distorted bodies below our feet

Like stepping stones to a beautiful idyllic place

Convinced that love isn't suicide

How you cried

Let your tears fall to the ground

Submerge all the hideousness

All the broken dreams and fallacies we don't believe

Nothing to misperceive

Like Adam and Eve

So I'll run my fingers through your blond strands

and get lost in the everlasting blue that is you

Never wanting to be found again

Let the misery dissipate

while the crooked snake's apple gets buried in the dirt

Let the seeds spring eternal and we'll breathe life into everything once again

FOR TODAY

I hear you crying out for help

I have no doubts

I'll shout

Hoping that you'll hear me one day

But you're still sharpening those knives

Longing for a bathtub to fill with your blood

and me, a lonely boy, that just wants to give you a hug

I just want to hear you laughing

Keep you safe and warm

I want my soul to be your refuge

Your salvation

What a disastrous situation

A world without your eyes is more than I can bear

Don't you see how much I care

or are you forever blind to everything that means something

I want to lick your wounds clean

Carry you on my back to the worlds beyond this one

When we're both ready

When the time is right

I'll hold your fragile hands steady

Please God, give me a sign that'll let me know it's not tonight

I'll stand up to the sun till I'm without sight

I won't give up this fight

Though I'm exhausted from flailing and failing

Ruminating on all the ways I'm waiting

Waiting for you to realize what you're truly worth

A rare angel on this earth

So don't leave us prematurely

Fathom the ways we love you purely

Even as you may tire of it all

Trying in futility to catch you as you fall

I beg don't give up or surrender

because I know everything can get better

If you just keep believing it

We'll transform these lies into dire truths

A transition like no other

You don't have to suffer

I'll find a way to mend your broken heart and your cracked insides

and we'll find a beautiful place to reside

Free from the anguish of the past

Forget all regrets and all the rest

Do it fast

Pummel them into the ground and stomp them out with your tiny feet

Like their on fire and only you can extinguish it

Don't let the flames ever consume you

As bright as they are

Let the embers blow away

Promise me, at least for today

HOW BRIGHT

Please let your tears wash away your pain as they splash down on this playground

As they tear down the memories of former children and their laughter

and replace it with—

Something more tragic

Something less certain

Something that will always remain

My love cannot protect you from the horrors of this world

My arms cannot lift this world from off your exhausted shoulders

but still I try and fail time and time again

My voice cannot calm your fears

My eyes cannot alleviate the traumas of your life

but still I try to be your savior

Your angel of life

Wanting to take you away from all of this misery and suffering

I'm your guardian

as weak as I may be

I'll be stronger for you

and I'll hold you with all my might

I'll never give up this fight

even as I lay here weeping beside you

And for some reason the demons won't let us rest

They keep cutting away at our souls

Trying to bury themselves in our holes

Making it so we have to crawl

and as my weary legs waver and my heart peters out

my last gasp will echo your name throughout this realm of darkness

for you are the only thing that brings light

Oh, and how bright . . . .

MY GODSEND

I have fallen into the darkest depths

Opaque and cold

Alone

and I'm reaching out longingly

Grasping onto false memories leading to wrong turns and dead-end roads

Saccharine and misplaced

Wanting a change of pace

I need to stare into a loving face

What a disgrace!

And everyone sees through me like I'm a ghost

Yearning to pass through floorboards or ceilings

Walls that have you sealed in like a prisoner

I'll haunt you till you realize my suffering is the same as yours

A martyr that dies for nothing and everything

Something

I'll curse the Gods above for not listening to my prayers

I'll question their very existence if I must

and wait for the Devil himself to appear like an apparition before me

May he take my hand

The prince of lies with his beady eyes and black horns

Yellow teeth from years of smoking

Can he read my soul like you once did

Like an open book with twists and turns revealing every idiosyncrasy

Every tormented step we've taken

and the blood on the pages is the same as theirs

Don't ever let yourself be forsaken

Find someone to cherish your name, your hair

If you dare . . .

Wear your blue eyes with pride

until all the negative feelings subside

and when you change into something more beautiful

Let the transformation stick

Yes, these feelings may make me sick

but it's what makes me tick

I'll walk this solitary path and crush the insects below my feet

With remorse deep in my heart I'll apologize

Will we rise

I'll look into you pious eyes and hope you're right

That you have the right kind of sight

An insight that leaves me dumbfounded

but no matter what

Whether there are pearly gates of white shinning bright

or a darkness the likes of no one's ever seen before

One thing is certain

Willingly and without hesitation I'll follow you to the end

For you must be my Godsend

COME DOWN

I can feel you in my blood and bones

Colliding against the particles of my soul

and yet I still feel alone

Can you fill this deep hole?

You're the one I call

to fill this ethereal void

or am I just someone you're meant to avoid

Call it a chore

like sneaking glances at you without you noticing at all

You are ever enticing

and when I wrap my arms around you

it's like holding a piece of heaven

I'll hold you up when you're feeling down

as long as you keep me around

and we won't ever let them pull this heaven below

where the demons lurk in the shadows

I make this powerful vow

and let the light filter through coalescing with your beauty

Expanding your mind and letting the evil spirits fade in obscurity

In desperation they'll cry for us

but we'll ignore their deafening pleas

and jump into the astonishing turquoise seas

I beg you please . . . .

Swim without a care in this world or the next

Let each wave caress your every pore

The moisture sticking to your skin and cleansing every inch

If I'm dreaming I beg don't give me a pinch

because I don't feel like waking up

and letting this memory of us falter and fade

We'll find a lovely place in the shade

Longing for your lips that may never come

even though I'd swim this ocean for you

and as my arms burn and everything feels like it's giving out

I'll swirl down if you weaken

and lift you up with my last ounce of strength

While you look to the wondrous sky

I'll slowly sink to the bottom

Hoping that when you've had your fill

You'll come down for me

Down this dark abyss

and we'll make any place we go pure bliss

FIND YOUR SELF

I have finally forgiven myself
For breathing you in like smoke
and coughing out remnants of our souls
Sending me to a purgatory so thick
Where I'm forever stuck and sick
I wade through it like it's syrup
and I know all I need is to touch your lips
Your clean and sweet labium
It'll send me on a trip
Out of this beckoning hell
There's promises down the line
I won't ever break them I can tell
Tearing down all the wrong way signs
Keeping us cruising the right way, the hardest way
and I'm still waiting for your smile to come my way
Sleeping silent soul come home and awaken
and let the light be the brightest I've ever seen
It won't ever be mistaken
My insides have been shaken
Since the very first time I laid eyes on you
As you circled the earth timidly
and I remember how God sent tears to your eyes
and how it burned inside to hear your cries

We both have scars stretching across our hearts

Jagged and rough incisions made from the darkest times in our lives

I'll struggle and tell you whose is worse

and I'll patch them up as best I can

Though it may sting at first

Just bear with the hurt

and we'll alleviate this hideous stain

The one that brings us to our knees over and over

We won't let it spread like a venomous virus

We'll stop this insane pain

Feign amnesia and forget that we don't know how to forget

No more lingering regrets

They just weigh us down like an anchor upon our chests

Crushing all that is beautiful within

So gaze into my eyes incapable of lies and get lost in them for once

Because I found myself in yours time and time again

YOU HAVE ME

I will sacrifice everyday

and all my life

for those red strands that blow in the wind

I want you to be my kind

Could it be a sign

When I hold you so close

and it feels so right

You shine like the brightest light

so instead of putting up a fight

just dance with it

I'll take the lead and make you smile for a while

Twirling as I do

We can spin and spin till we're dizzy from circling the world

Inside me you can curl

I'll always keep you safe and warm

and you can say what you want to say

and I'll try to say what I need to say

Swallow me like a pill that doesn't make you choke

That makes you feel good and keeps your soul from shaking

This atrocious trepidation that takes over when you least expect

I'll promise you I'm not faking

This fallacy, this horrid love bringing me to my knees that won't ever let me get up

I long to find that one hand that is willing to help me stand on these quaking knees

Your glorious ears that truly listen to me speak

when I'm feeling incredibly weak

Could it be you I seek?

I just need you closer

Smother me like I'm on fire

Like a trick birthday candle flicking off and on over and over

Don't let me feed off the purple air

Beware!

There's poison all around

It's in our pores

I'll suck it out as best I can and replace it with an inevitable kiss

and a daring wish I'll make while I loose my wits

Let me be all you'll ever need

I'll always take heed

and when we proceed

Hand in Hand I hope

We'll carve a path with our feet

and we won't ever be beat

like I always imagined it could be

so close your eyes so you can finally see

All along you had me

HERE TO STAY

My heart skips a beat

when you are near

I'll chase you like a dog in heat

I have ascertained

You're the one I seek

and it's branded across my face

What I would do for a tiny taste

Look into my eyes and see your beautiful reflection

Even though you'll never know how you've made my world quake

looking into you're ever changing eyes full of dejection

and if you knew, the question is: what would you do?

A fond farewell to a series of rejections

Wanting to start over new with you

I want to get caught some how in your long lashes

I'll struggle to find a way

and I'll look at the world in a thousand new ways

Forgetting the ghosts that haunt us with their pail misery

Like the one I passed through

and the one you held knives to

Let's forget the past for once and look into our respective futures

May they be bright like a jesus night light

and though my scars are held loosely by sutures

I hope you can mend them while I fix every one of yours

Delicate and intricate

Give me this diligent chore

and I'll do my best not to mess it up this time

I know now that loving beauty is not a crime

I'll give you the tallest mountain to climb

and when we reach that peak

that special place that no one can take away from us

burning in our hearts

Illuminating the devious dark

Together above it all we'll stand

and I'll shyly reach for your hand

Frail like a white dove floating in the ocean skies

and with this confession I'll break through all the lies

Surprise!

I'm here to stay

though it may drive me crazy

I'm here to stay

because I know I'd plunge into deeper depths of madness if you went away

LOST AND FOUND

When I sleep I dream of you

You know these feelings are true

and there's no use trying to deny them

and there's no 12 step program to help me get over you

I won't ever walk down those steps unless you ask me to

and you know I'd just tumble down recklessly

Yes, you've penetrated the inside of my mind

and I'll leave you there unconfined

and when you're near me I can hardly take how you shine

It's leaves me in a bind

Going blind

and the darkness I see is beautiful like you

I want it to envelop me

Wrap me up and keep me safe

The way I want to get you tangled in my arms

You know I won't ever bring you harm

You leave me disarmed

With no weapons to fight with

Though I know I don't have much fight left

So lay you're hands on me

and I'll surrender to you completely

Weakly

Just stay within reach

Something I'll beseech

Because I want to be yours

and you can be everything I need in my life

And in these dreams we can be whatever we want to be

Don't you see?

We can make these dreams a reality

Underneath these pink clouds we can see infinity

and hold hands under the glorious skyline

An aching need to touch you skin that leaves me dazed

It's almost enough to bring me to my knees and ask God to do me a favor

Just let it work out this time

Please put your hand in mine

and tell me you feel something, anything

Could I feel it enough for the both of us

This incredible rush

like adrenalin pumping through my veins before I jump off the tallest building

Can you break my fall?

This maddening descent into oblivion

Fill the void with your effulgent essence

It's your presence

So please stay around

and I'll do my best not to keep you down

I beg pick me up out of the lost and found

RAVAGE MY SOUL

Take me to the infinity in your eyes
where there's nothing to despise
tears come from your whimpering cries
and it makes me weak
it burns in the pit of my stomach
and I've been warned repeatedly
to not let you break my heart
Don't leave me in the overwhelming dark
I've been here for too damn long
Bemoaning past loves that have left me
Can't I see, it's not them that represent me
I am so much more
and I can be yours for cheap
Drag me around in a heap
or Sheppard me like I'm a sheep
because I need you
These feelings are real
I bet you didn't know that they were a part of the deal
Did you ever make one with God, begging for someone
I know I use to pray for someone to come along
and fate sat me right in front of you
Through all the twists and turns I've been through

I found myself before you

Don't you see by now how I adore you

How I dream of taking you in my arms and kissing your divine lips

It's etched in my mind from the surreal

and now that I've have nothing left to conceal

I feel like I'm floating on the air

A feeling I want you to share

Is it something you wouldn't dare let your self feel

I know we can make it if we take it slow

We'll destroy all our foes and know . . . .

The future can be what we make it

Something almost as bright as your glorious soul

though nothing can match it

Nothing can out shine or dilute it

While mine feels used and rusty

from the wear and tear of bygone years

though you have nothing to fear

Within me there's a gaping hole

So feel free anytime, anywhere to ravage my soul